Godsight

Crossway books by Lael Arrington

Worldproofing Your Kids
Godsight: Renewing the Eyes of Our Hearts

LAEL ARRINGTON

RENEWING THE EYES OF
OUR HEARTS

Godsight

CROSSWAY BOOKS

A PUBLISHING MINISTRY OF
GOOD NEWS PUBLISHERS
WHEATON, ILLINOIS

Godsight

Copyright © 2005 by Lael Arrington

Published by Crossway Books
        a publishing ministry of
        Good News Publishers
        1300 Crescent Street
        Wheaton, Illinois 60187

Cover design: Josh Dennis

Cover photo: Getty Images

First printing 2005

Printed in the United States of America

Unless otherwise designated, Scripture is taken from *The Holy Bible, English Standard Version*. Copyright © 2001 by Crossway Bibles, a publishing ministry of Good News Publishers. Used by permission. All rights reserved.

Scripture designated NIV is taken from the *Holy Bible: New International Version®*. Copyright © 1973, 1978, 1984 by International Bible Society. Used by permission of Zondervan Publishing House. All rights reserved. The "NIV" and "New International Version" trademarks are registered in the United States Patent and Trademark Office by International Bible Society. Use of either trademark requires the permission of International Bible Society.

Scripture quotations marked MSG are taken from *The Message*. Copyright © 2002. Used by permission of NavPress Publishing Group.

Library of Congress Cataloging-in-Publication Data

Arrington, Lael F., 1951-
   Godsight : renewing the eyes of our hearts / Lael Arrington.
      p. cm.
   ISBN 1-58134-632-8
   1. Spiritual life—Christianity. I. Title.
BV4501.3.A775   2005
248.4—dc22   2005004961

RRDH		15	14	13	12	11	10	09	08	07	06	05
15	14	13	12	11	10	9	8	7	6	5	4	3	2	1

To Zach

our back-porch poet
and musician extraordinaire,
our greatest gift from God

Your imagination delights my soul.

For resources and information on
Lael Arrington's ministry
please visit
www.laelarrington.com
or for booking contact
Speak Up Speaker Services
888-870-7719

CONTENTS

1

CAN YOU EVEN
IMAGINE?

We shall be as a City upon a Hill . . .
we must be knit together in this work as one man.
JOHN WINTHROP'S LAY SERMON ON THE PURITAN FLAGSHIP
BOUND FOR AMERICA

I just want to feel good, don't want to hurt nobody.
I just want to get a good time out of my life.
ALTERNATIVE ROCKER BOB SCHNEIDER, "CAPTAIN KIRK"

If you could edit together a highlights reel of your imagination—snippets of your fondest dreams—what would it look like? Would it be your own signature version of the American dream, a founding-father epic vision of building a better life, becoming the "best you" you can be, striving from goal to goal? A *Seinfeld/Friends* one-day-at-a-time-sized series featuring a tight circle of kindred spirits who shrug and smile together at life's slings and arrows? Some comfortable but slightly more energetic suburban dream in-between? What about when you were younger? How did the imagination of your youth feed the dreams of your future? I've never sold tickets, but there's always been quite a show playing on the screen of my imagination.

The earliest was a dollhouse soap opera where the mother fell down the stairs, and the father fell off the roof, and the baby fell off the balcony, and the pink-dressed little girl jumped off everything to save them so many times that her arm fell off. It made her life so painful and yet ever more heroic, like I wanted to be.

As I grew older, the curtain closed on the dollhouse and opened on Barbie. Somehow the plots always revolved around Barbie needing to change clothes. The more outfits she had, the more elaborate the story. In a clothes-driven plot, the scenes you can play are limited by the outfits you have available. So it took a great deal of shopping and sewing to keep the series on the air.

But the Barbie stories had to alternate showings with my horses. We didn't own a horse, although my mother offered to buy me a burro. I don't think she understood the horse movies in my head. A burro could never serve as understudy for the Black Stallion. When I ran out of Walter Farley's books, I wrote my own. I used my mother's spoons to dig a maze of tunnels in the island dirt of my backyard so my plastic stallion could hide his mares from the thieving intruders that washed ashore.

I played the organ and guitar, but there was rarely a time when I practiced alone in the living room. I played for audiences of thousands. That's why scales were a nonstarter. What audience wants to hear scales when they are breathlessly waiting to hear "I Could Have Danced All Night"?

When I was a child, I imagined as a child. When I became a teenager, I put away childish imagination. I shifted from present-tense fantasy play to future-tense reality movies. College . . . marriage . . . home and family—the Beach Boys sang the sound track—"Wouldn't it be nice?" to be older so we could be married and not have to say goodnight—a refreshing lyric for today's world. I can remember praying soft little pleading prayers: "Oh, Lord, I love you, but please don't let Jesus return until I get married."

And then I *was* married and surveying the late-basement, early-Holiday Inn decor of our first home with the eyes of budget-busting imagination. I could just see the new wallpaper, new couch, new chairs, new coffee table. Then I had a child and began producing his future-tense movie.

In my professional life the youth leader in me dreamed of being the cool first-year teacher who would attract kids like free pizza. And they came, partying in my room, hanging off the rafters until my new dream was to teach just one orderly, uninterrupted lesson. College faculty, conference speaker, author—the titles I aspired to opened one door after another into sacred circles of which I had dreamed of being a part.

As I sit here in my dark study sipping cherry limeade and watching old reruns of *House Beautiful* dreams and Barbie fantasies, something wells up in my chest—*gratitude!* I am astonished at how God has changed my dreams. I have spent all the life I remember as a child of the King. But until the more recent past, the dreams that played in my imagination were not, for the most part, his highest. I see a girl, a teen, a young woman whose imagination was much less enthralled by God and his kingdom than by what C. S. Lewis calls "the evil enchantment of worldliness." Only it didn't look evil because it was such a nice Christian variation on the American dream of success.

For as long as I can remember, I've known the gospel story. God has always been the foundation of my life. But foundations don't inspire movies. The plotlines in my head, my dreams, the best of everything I could imagine was downsized by the enchanted voice that whispers, *The life you want most is here in this world. The nice family, good job, fun weekends, lovely home, two cars, friends to enjoy it with—it's all here. Even a nice church.*

If God was the foundation of my life, then the unseen reality of God's kingdom was the wallpaper. Enjoyable. Comforting. Neatly covering the walls of my world, wrapping around me in times of need, but mostly it was just there. Served as a nice background on which to hang the big plasma screen of my imagination. The stories that played on it were more often about making a good life here than building a kingdom. To me they seemed one and the same.

Most of the characters in my movies were Christians. We loved God. But you might not see much of a spark of passion in our eyes or hear an intensity of desire in our voices when we talked about him.

We went to church and Christian camps and conferences. But we did not wake up thinking, *Today we have a kingdom to build. Thy kingdom come, Lord, one cup of water at a time, one listening ear at a time, as we pour ourselves into building the one thing that lasts with the trowel and mortar of our gifts.*

We enjoyed studying our Bibles, but we did not see our lives as playing a significant part in a continuing story that stretches back to the cross and before that to creation, and sweeps past us to end in the defeat of God's enemies and our wedding party with the Lover of our souls.

And lost people? Occasionally my dreams and passion would be directed toward rescuing the hurting or deceived. Not too many plots centered on my personal, heart-to-heart involvement with the one listening to the truth I had to offer.

I wonder if what we have here, in my life, in the lives of other sincere Christians, in an age absolutely glutted with powerful images, is a failure of imagination. In a popular passage from "The Weight of Glory," C. S. Lewis wrote: "If we consider the staggering nature of the rewards promised . . . it would seem that our Lord finds our desires not too strong, but too weak. We are half-hearted creatures, fooling about with drink and sex and ambition when infinite joy is offered us, like an ignorant child who wants to go on making mud pies in a slum because *he cannot imagine* what is meant by the offer of a holiday at the sea" (emphasis mine).[1]

And it doesn't have to be mud pies in the slum, although I've made my share. A nice Christian life of playing sensibly in your yard still doesn't compare to a holiday at the sea. Somehow we can grow up in Christian families and good churches and still find ourselves unable to imagine the beauty, wonder, and splendor of God and his dreams for us.

Our imaginations are starved for Godsight.

Like righteous Job we are wonder challenged.

While we strolled the mall one evening with our friends Leighton and Karen, discussing the latest in Cabela's camouflage and the meaning of life, Leighton asked me, "Of what did Job repent?"

I thought of Job's litany of intense loss and physical pain. I remembered how, at the end of Job's story, God showed him the full measure of his majesty and the glory of his heart poured out in creation, and I recalled Job's halting, awestruck response: "Surely I spoke of things I did not understand, things too wonderful for me to know."

Leighton tucked the scene into a neat little phrase: "His wonder was too small."

Our failure of desire for God and his kingdom naturally flows from a failure of imagination of the splendor and beauty of our rewards, our promised kingdom, and the God who gives them and himself to us as gifts.

Perhaps, like me, you could say you grew up with a passion for God's truth. In churches with a modern mind-set perhaps we over-dosed on TMI—too much information. Strong on the lectures, weak on the missional labs. But perhaps, like mine, your imagination has been so focused on knowing God's Word and doing his commands that you can miss the glory of his pictures and his story. Your mind pro-cesses the information, but it doesn't stir your passion. You believe things, really believe things in your head. But the reality doesn't flow out of your heart, and you wonder why your time with God is scattered and pleasant at best, boring at worst.[2]

You may even find yourself in a place where hope has given way to resignation, the fizz of delight for God and life has faded into a warm, flat glass of duty. You can't imagine what it would take to get the sparkle back; so you are settling for living small. Perhaps you even find yourself escaping that small place, pouring what you vaguely suspect might be too much energy into good-life dreams, entertainment, and fantasies—the "safe" distractions that stay privately confined to our screens and imagination.

Maybe your imagination has always romped in fields of entertain-ment and shopping dreams. Perhaps your vision is lasered in on how to make your quota or finish your degree. Or maybe you are focused on relationships and the care of the soul. You dream of being a good friend, good wife, good parent.

No matter what images are playing in your imagination, maybe the shows of family, career, and entertainment have taken over the entire screen, squeezing out the pictures of something bigger and higher that you long to be a part of. You yearn for a larger mission in life, but you get lost in the dailiness of all the mess that work and school and people track into your life.

Perhaps, rather than dreams and dailiness, your imagination is gripped by fears that add terror to terror—the homeland security kind or perhaps the domestic terror of abandonment, the waywardness of a child. Perhaps just the specter of another lonely weekend stalks your quiet moments. You long for a peace and a Presence that deeply comforts.

Brent Curtis and John Eldredge remind us in *The Sacred Romance* that we need a new way of seeing, that "desire is kept alive by imagination—the antidote to resignation." If your imagination and desire for God and the kingdom kind of life need an infusion of light and color and passion, then I invite you to Godsight—an opening of the eyes of the heart, a study and an experience of how God can grow our vision, our new way of seeing him and his kingdom.

This book is about how God takes the vision for life we absorb from our families, our group, the American dream, Oprah, Hollywood, and even our modern church programs so focused on Bible study and activities—God takes this vision and begins to refocus our mud-pie imagination to see the glory of his holiday-at-the-sea. *Godsight* is about how God shows himself to us and exchanges our dreams for his dreams . . .

> . . . through the pain he allows,
> . . . through the enablement to choose his dreams
>   when everything within us wants our own,
> . . . through the people he sends to cast his vision into our lives,
> . . . through a renewed mission of taking Jesus to the world,
> . . . through seeking him with intensity and finding him face to
>   face,
> . . . through a refreshed vision of eternity.

Along the way I offer the story of my own journey—not because I have such an extraordinary tale to tell but because God looks so good in the telling of it. And because the way God has captured my imagination and changed my dreams is a case study deeply true to Scripture of how he shows himself to us . . .

> . . . though the emptiness of achieving our small dreams,

. . . through the pain of losing the dreams that he denies,

. . . through the discovery of our highest dreams enfolded
within his larger dreams of kingdom mission.

Of course no eyes, including mine, have really seen or fully imagined the wonder of God or the holiday at the sea, but we catch glimpses through the dark glass. In these pages I want to hand you the night-vision goggles and point out more places to look.

We will take a creative look at how the seductive images that surround us shrink-wrap our *vision*. We'll turn our imaginations to the infinitely terrible beauty of God on the throne, God on the cross. We are so oblivious to the unseen half of the universe. We need the big-bang and big-burn visions, metaphors, parables, and drama of the prophets to smack our imaginations: "Hey! Snap out of it! What does this mean for you?"

We'll take a look at our own private field of dreams—our daydreams and fantasies and the hours we spend in front of our screens. We'll ask the right questions like, *What does it matter if the life we enjoy in distraction and fantasy isn't real?* We'll compare our dreams to what the Bible tells us about both God's dreams and Satan's dreams and think about the direction in which our own dreams are moving. We'll discover some answers from God's Word together. I'll share with you some answers I've learned on my journey. Others you will find on your own.

Nothing fires our imaginations like a good story because we were made to be a part of one. This book is a deeper imagining of God's kingdom story, the one that has always been my sure foundation. My fallback position. But what does it really mean to my everyday life? How does an understanding of God's story connect my heart to his? We'll see how the setting, characters, plotline, flashbacks, and suspense that God has scripted show us his heart. How that vision can ignite our passion to live our crucial role and free us from living small and distracted. How it can deliver us from the daily taffy pull between what our hearts want over here and what God wants over there, leaving our souls feeling thin and stringy in the middle.

More than an account of my journey, what follows is an invitation to make your own journey . . .

Beyond the goodness of duty
　to the richness of desire.
From living small in distraction and resignation,
　to living large in God's kingdom story.
Beyond the beauty of seeking God's truth so our minds can understand,
　to the fullness of seeking his face so our hearts can worship.
From the indulgence of our illusions
　to the reformation of our imaginations.
It is an invitation to Godsight.

We collectors of diplomas and degrees tend to exalt the queen of reason and banish imagination and emotion, like unruly stepchildren, to the cellar of our souls. Like C. S. Lewis we may feel the threat of an imagination that "far exceeds (our) obedience." In *Mere Christianity* he wrote, "It is not reason that is taking away my faith; on the contrary, my faith is based on reason. It is my imagination and emotions. The battle is between faith and reason on one hand and emotion and imagination on the other."[3]

For the longest time I thought Christianity was about turning off the bad pictures and tamping down the negative emotions, bolting them behind the cellar door and doing my duty. God wired me to be more of a thinker than a feeler, and I focused on living, loving, and teaching worldview from the head. But God and life have taught me what that great New England preacher Jonathan Edwards once observed, "The nature of human beings is to be inactive unless influenced by some affection: love, hatred, desire, hope, fear, etc. These affections are the spring of action." It's true.

We live from our affections—our desire, our passion.

Our imaginations stir our desires, and our desires make our lives go 'round. They write checks on our bank accounts and entries into our day-timers.

We ignore the power of turning our imagination toward God at our peril.

Every child of God experiences the tension between two warring realms of the imagination: Satan wants us to focus on imaginary fears or our dreams of rising in influence and importance in a material world we can see and touch. God invites us to imagine, with the eyes of our hearts, the reality of his life and kingdom, both now and especially in the future. We don't need to just turn off the bad pictures.

We need Godsight—a refreshed, renewed, redeemed imagination for our journey.

What I've been able to see, I have desired. That vision has touched my heart and moved me to action. If we look through Hebrews 11, we can't miss the way the living-color vision of people like Abraham and Moses moved them to leave the comforts of the ancient Near East suburbs and palaces to seek a City, to look for their reward. Or perhaps we can miss it if we don't really take the time to enter their stories in our imaginations . . .

In the heat of the day, Abraham sat at the entrance to his tent listening to the children's laughter rippling out from his servants' tents. Sarah heard it too and caught his eye, silent as a stone. Slowly she stood up and paused, giving her worn-out joints time to settle; then she disappeared through the flap behind him. Abraham rose and drifted over the empty ground surrounding his tent. His hips ached, and his forearms, he noticed, were still shrinking beneath his spotted, crinkly hide. He straightened, shaking the dust out of his robe, and stared into the middle distance. Through the shimmering glare he could see the City, gates open. A huge City on massive, multiple foundations. It would have to be great to welcome the millions whom God promised would bear a part of his soul. His eyes settled again upon the vacant lots. But his ears heard the laughter that would crack the emptiness and gush life into their tent.

It was the splash of Isaac's laughter he remembered years later, as he sweated up the mountain in Moriah. Playing with the servants' children. Telling stories by the fire. Laughter mixed with awe the night the meteors streaked past the moon.

A few steps ahead, his boy's bare arms glistened in the heat, the wood for the sacrifice strapped on his back. And if God didn't break in? His ears strained, listening for a rescue, an alternative to what waited at the top of this rock. Could he plunge his knife into that laughing throat? If he could, would God stop the bleeding? Breathe life back into that body?

Abraham's gaze glanced off the knife tucked in his belt and reached past the boy's head to the City. Though distant, it was more real than the look in Isaac's eyes when he raised his knife.

From the far side of the Nile Moses looked back at the sun setting behind Pharaoh's palace, backlighting the massive buildings, radiating gold halos from the stone heads of Ra and Osiris. Slaves emerged from the palace and, in a slow, almost choreographed fire dance, worked their way down both sides of the giant staircase, lighting torches that sparkled off the gold trim on the columns and the royal barge tethered below. The rays reached for him, and the breeze brushed his face with the aroma of fine wines and sizzling meats. First a trickle, then a steady stream of Egypt's finest floated down between the columns to the water's edge, the women in their gauzy cotton gowns and gold crescent jewelry, his brothers baring their strength and watching the women.

Turning, Moses stared at the huts of the Hebrews squatting on the edge of the wilderness. Caught in the full illumination of the sunset, their mud and straw bricks swallowed the light whole. Not a crumb of glimmer to draw him. For forty years of privilege his complete incuriosity about the people in those huts had been proof that he belonged. But he bore their mark, and that mark was connecting him not just to the weary faces, but to a rising Presence who loved those faces. He dropped his head and raked the dusty ground with his sandal. Beyond the huts, in the recesses of the darkening eastern sky, the invisible One held out a calling and a promise that blazed more brightly than the treasures behind him. Moses drew a deep breath and made his way toward the huts.

We live by faith. Faith sees things that are unseen, seen only in our imaginations. We remember and are comforted and inspired by God's great works in the past. When my manuscript due date is barreling down the tracks, and I'm frozen in the headlight, blinking and wondering how little sleep does it really take to keep thinking and writing, I am comforted by the remembrance that on a deadline past God miraculously healed my fizzled computer, and just weeks ago he protected my life in a wreck that totaled my car. And I am deeply grateful. But faith is what carries me to the next deadline.

Faith is future-oriented. "The evidence of things hoped for." It imagines and believes all that God will be for us in the next few moments, tomorrow, and in our future life, reigning with Christ forever. Most of what we hope and long for is yet to come. Most of the joy God holds out for us is still "set before us," in the future. In *Future Grace*, John Piper says, "The key to faith's power is that it embraces the future grace promised by God and is more satisfied with this than the pleasures promised by sin."

The heroes of Hebrews 11 were sure and absolutely certain of God's promises. With the eyes of his heart, in his faith-lit imagination, Abraham could see the future City, opening its gates to his family, too large to count. Moses could see his future reward from the One who is invisible. I read their stories and think, *How would my life be different if I could see God like Moses did? Or see the City like Abraham could?*

For instance, picture yourself looking around at lunchtime traffic. Without a flying De Lorean it will be impossible to get everything done. You begin re-ranking your to-do list on the "tyranny of the urgent" scale. The gas tank bell dings again for the #1 spot, and your cell phone pleads for a substitution.

Driving from #2 to #3, you take the bottom ranked items off the lunchtime to-do list and insert them at the top of your on-the-way-home list. You replay your mental voice messages, while the radio commercials compete for your attention:

I need a clean uniform . . .

Buy me . . .

Your father's PSA count shot up . . .

We'd love for you to lead a small group . . .

Please, buy me . . .

Your pictures are ready . . .

Hey, can you take us to the . . .

BUY ME, BUY ME, BUY ME . . .

As you drive along in the midst of your lists and your dailiness and the voices peddling their vision of the good life, what if you could look up and see not the glare of the sun, but the glow of a City much closer than the sun? What if you could see the Shekinah glory of God reflecting off a magnificent skyline of golden buildings shimmering in the rainbow radiance John described in Revelation 21, rising above their topaz, emerald, sapphire, and amethyst foundations? What if you could sit at the stoplight and look up over the traffic to see it suspended in the sky, more real than the moon or the sun? Watch the ripples and pulses of its living radiance the way you watch the flicker of a candle in a distant window?

Can you even imagine?

Or picture yourself walking into the empty homestead after the funeral of a widowed grandparent. You tour the rooms of your family museum that echo with the hum of conversation and dishwashing clatter after family feasts and the laughter as you and your cousins jumped on the beds. You tour the collections of your grandmother's treasures: teacups, spoons, and everybody's "paintings," including your pathetic paint-by-number kitten that she actually framed and hung. And something rises in your throat because you suspect (you really know but you can't admit to such finality), you suspect that this is the last time this family will be together under this roof. At some point you'll return with your children or your brother to rescue the things you love and even many lesser treasures from the second death of the estate sale, but this is the final gathering in.

What if the family could draw together on the back porch one last time and look up and see the City shimmering in the twilight? What if you could sit in the old swing and fix your eyes upon it and see where your granddad was, present with the King? Would the grownups point out the wall and foundations and the great pearl gates that never shut? Would the children smile up at the City and wave and blow kisses across the miles?

Can you even imagine?

Abraham and Moses could. They lived extraordinary lives of purpose, risk, and impact because they could see God and their future with the eyes of faith. Their imaginations played movies of God's promises.

When, from the God-breathed words of Scripture and the depth of our worship and prayers, we catch a vision of God's beauty shining into a heart that wants to obey, we build a kingdom. We chase a city. We do the things our heroes did in Hebrews 11.

I've rarely seen people in Scripture who, when they saw the reality of the majesty and beauty of God, didn't give up their own vision of life and sign on to build his kingdom. I've rarely seen anyone who, like an Isaiah or an Ezekiel, saw the throne and heard the voice like rushing waters and afterwards spent their lives sort of diddling around, playing video games or hanging out at the mall. From Abraham to Moses, Daniel to Paul, those who could see it were enthralled. Their passion ignited. From the wellspring of their affections flowed great actions in the kingdom story.

God has changed my dreams from black-and-white 8mm's of playing "mud pies in the slum" to a Technicolor omni-vision of a "holiday at the sea" with him. He wants to do the same thing for you. His Spirit wants to take God's pictures and story and do a miracle—show us the Father's heart and bind our hearts to his and, like the heroes of our faith, lift us above the dailiness of our lives and inspire us with the same passion and purpose.

I've lived far too much of my life under "the evil enchantment of worldliness" where the monotony of my to-do lists or the chronic hurt of my illness or my smaller dreams of being a "success" crowd my screen. In his mercy the King breaks in with Godsight—pictures of the holiday at the sea. Pictures of his kingdom story come to dispel the enchantment and grab my heart.

Can you even imagine?

2

DREAM SEEKERS

The Cosmic Blonde floats through life on a beam of sunshine,
from success to success.
COMIC SOCIOLOGIST DAVID BROOKS

When we can't imagine something, how do we move forward? A first-rate imaginer, *Star Wars* writer and producer George Lucas has said, "Dreams are extremely important. You can't do it unless you imagine it."

In America we are nurtured from the crib with dreams of aspiration and progress. We tend to catch the Puritan vision of building that "City on the Hill" that the intervening eighteen generations have deconstructed to mean the relentless pursuit of happiness in a lifestyle suited to our own radically individual tastes. It may look like a gated enclave of McMansions with a view for some, a home schooling co-op for others. Even when our families and churches cast a clear biblical vision of God and his rainbow-foundationed city, we can have a hard time seeing it in high definition because we simultaneously receive such dazzling pictures of the "evil enchantment of worldliness," American dreams of "success," and the desires of our own divided hearts.

But God is relentlessly at work redeeming our imaginations so that we'll see the glory of his heart and his kingdom and embrace his dreams as our own. Perhaps you'll recognize his fine-tuning of your own dreams as I show you how he has changed mine.

I'm a born tap dancer and grew up a Cosmic Blonde.

I love the image of tap dancing for performing. That face that remains smiling and still while arms and legs wind up into a blur of motion. I grew up tap dancing with one foot in God's Kingdom Story and one foot in my own small performance story, the story Shakespeare wrote about when he said, "All the world's a stage." The performance storyline says, "Life really *is* a stage. If I'm pretty and smart enough and tap-dance well enough, I'll be a star."

The way David Brooks explains it in his book *On Paradise Drive* (with deep apologies to anyone whose hair happens to be blonde), a "Cosmic Blonde" is a condition of the soul—jet-skiing along the surface of life, oblivious to the deeper meanings of the story or motivations of the heart. I tap-danced my way through my childhood, youth, and early adult years, self-satisfied, book-smart but unreflective, and enjoying the party of life. The one who brought home the English honors but hated to write because it took time away from the party. The "simple" soul in Proverbs on a winning streak. Perhaps a lot of us grow up a little Blonde.

Some of my story is not easy to share. It tells of shallow aspirations and deep longings to feel accepted and invited into the inner circle. I knew that God loved me, but he seemed to be out there on the back row. From my vantage point upon the stage, I've been much more attuned to the approval on faces on the front row—parents, friends, husband, community.

I come from a Christian clan, a very churched Cosmic Blonde. Like the apostle Paul's young friend Timothy, my faith was passed down from my grandmothers to my parents to me. One of my first visitors in the hospital nursery was my pastor. I couldn't wait until I was old enough to go to Christian camp. Beside the horse books and Oz books on my shelf stood missionary biographies of *Mary Slessor* and *Borden of Yale*. Every few years my great-aunt and uncle returned from Thailand with tales of real-life missionary adventures. Maybe there were too many stories about lizards and snakes because their sold-out-to-the-kingdom dreams didn't grab my heart.

A brilliant Rhodes scholar, my pastor taught the Bible with charisma and authority and inspired me with a passion for God's truth. We studied God like we studied other doctrines, lining out his character in solid theological chunks of sovereignty, eternal life, love, truth, and lots of omni's. The picture I remember is one of a mighty God full of grace. I grew up in Psalm 119—delighting in the precepts and principles. But the story seemed distant—ancient and future, not present. And my heart longed for fun and excitement. Now. My passion for truth as ideas and precepts didn't translate into *passion* for a *Person*.

That's not to say I didn't know and love Jesus.

I prayed. Prayed to receive Christ as my Savior at the pastor's invitation after the sermon at the age of five. Prayed to trust him as Savior at a revival at my cousin's church. Prayed to do it again a few more times after that. You know, when you are so small and God is so big, I never was quite sure I got my arms around him. Did I really understand the depth and majesty of this redemption thing at age five? Well, just in case . . . I would pray again. Although my serial repentance probably flowed from the natural growth process of a maturing mind and heart, I think even then my lack of vision for the kingdom life took its toll. I was so focused on being on the right side of that line of faith rather than entering a new kind of life with Jesus.

Finally I remember leaning against the doorjamb of my bedroom when I was twelve. *Lord, if I never understood it or made the connection before, this is IT. I know I'm a sinner. I know Christ died for me. And I receive your forgiveness and your gift of eternal life. I trust you with my life. And this really is IT. I'm not praying this again. Amen.*

And I didn't. I have grown up with the confidence that I am loved and forgiven.

One of my earliest dreams was to wear a Princess crown in the "King's Daughters' Court" at summer camp. You could knock out Maid in a week and stand there glowing in the Friday night campfire in your good dress and red sequined crown. Duchess took longer. And Princess took years. But if you could read the whole Bible and memorize *all* of Isaiah 53 and Romans 8, a magnificent jeweled gold crown was gently lowered onto your head.

I wish I could say that I truly caught a vision at camp for what it meant to be a princess in my Father's kingdom. I did catch glimpses from a circle of people who loved Jesus and loved kids. I learned a lot of God's Word. But a part of my heart just wanted those crowns.

I've grown up in a culture that worships performance and the jet fuel that makes it go—ambition. For as long as I could tap-dance, I have felt the tension between my ambition to perform well and my aspiration to love and honor God. My story is one of being uniquely gifted and struggling to find that place in the kingdom where my gifts and talents could be poured out for him. It's a story of letting the applause and attention go and *wanting* to pour out my gifts and talents in kingdom service.

By the time I finished junior high, my dream was to be a high school star. I remember walking into the main hall my freshman year before the first bell and passing the glass cage of a giant stuffed grizzly bear, our mangy but fierce school mascot. I wanted to gather in front of the bear where the in-crowd gathered. I remember pushing my tray down the cafeteria line with one eye on the tables where sat the cheer-leaders, football players, and the rest of our high school glitterati. I wanted to sit in the sacred circle.

I had a baseline, foundational commitment to God and church. I had a passion for Bible study and learning truth. I loved Young Life where we did Bible study with cute guys. Mine was such a divided heart. If you could have stuck a passion thermometer in the part of my heart that wanted God, it wouldn't have shot the mercury up nearly as high as the part that wanted fun and friendships. I wanted to be noticed. But I didn't want to just be noticed, like great wallpaper. *I wanted to be chosen.*

And eventually I was. I gathered in front of the bear. Ate lunch in the sacred circle. I was voted secretary of the student council. My boyfriend was voted head cheerleader. In the small world of high school I was tap-dancing on center stage. They even pinned the fairy tale Most Beautiful crown on my head and laid the sheaf of glorious roses in my arms.

But as the night of the beauty pageant wore on, a curious thing happened. The applause drained away. There I was at the very pinna-cle of my high school dreams, watching my best friend and runner-up,

Judy, leave with her boyfriend. My boyfriend and I had parted company, and so I left with my parents for ice cream at my uncle's house. I heard Peggy Lee's song even though the stereo wasn't on. "Is that all there is? Is that all there is? . . ." Being chosen and even crowned somehow wasn't enough. The needle on my heart-tank fell to empty.

If someone had said to me, "Lael, life is a battle for God's kingdom, and your heart was made to delight in God; crowns are never enough," I doubt if my Blonde soul would have even known how to process the information. I lived the Baby Boomer good life on a street named Suburbia. My friends nicknamed me Lael Hi Skool. I couldn't have been more churched unless I spent my date nights there. (Actually our church did run a Friday night Bible study. *Study?* Friday night *was* date night.) I thought I loved God with all my heart. But I didn't see a picture of God that truly meant more than being crowned and applauded, even though I could taste the emptiness of that moment on stage.

I thought of Judy leaving with her boyfriend and wondered, *Who won and who lost?* I supposed that what I really needed was to be chosen by a special guy. I was a queen without a king. Even at seventeen I longed for Prince Charming and Happily Ever After.

About the time I touched the emptiness of my high school dreams, I graduated and left for the University of Texas at Austin—a big, new stage for an ambitious tap dancer. I thrived in the academic environment, but my Cosmic Blonde heart lived for the social scene.

Although I loved to study and learn, I had little vision for a career. None of the women in my family or church talked careers or mission, except for the aunt with the snakes in Thailand. Aside from a secretary here and a teacher there, none of the women had careers. They dreamed of being wives and moms. They were wives and moms, with a godly mission to raise their children, go to church, and enjoy family and friends.

When I broke up with a fellow I was dating, I took my broken heart out to the Christian camp of my youth and sat atop a windswept hill thinking, *Ah, Lord God, this Prince Charming thing is so hard. I can't make it happen, and I've got to shift my focus. I've been a sponge all my life. Just soaking up all your blessings. It's high time I become a channel— start really giving to others.* It was a choice made more out of desperation than a vision of God and his kingdom. But I've found that God meets us in those decisions either way. Throughout my life he's had this habit of tearing up the script of my small Cosmic Blonde Tap Dancer story and pulling me further into his. In one of those lovely kingdom "coincidences," I was invited to volunteer with a Young Life club.

In our Young Life leadership group I had my first taste of community built around a vision for ministry, and my focus for what I wanted in life was forever enlarged. Our mission, and boy did we have one, was to begin a new Young Life club in a fairly new high school. We began our "contact work"—getting to know students to invite them to club— at a football game in a hurricane. Our umbrellas blew inside out, the rain pelted, and the students wondered, "Who are these crazy college kids who would come to a football game in a torrent and want to meet us?" We saw kids saved, a ministry started, and along the way I met another club leader with whom I shared more than ministry. Sometimes you land in the middle of something that is so much larger than any vision you ever imagined. The friendships last a lifetime. And the memories . . .

Seeing God use you to bring kids to Christ and grow them up in their faith

Praying together and seeing God answer

Fifties party, moonlight sailing, and peanut butter willies . . .

Sadly, the next year the vision crumbled. A new Young Life director wanted to shake up the leadership. I thought I had found the young man of my dreams. When we broke up, I threw myself onto God who loved me enough to tear up another page of my small story and woo me more deeply into his. I continued as a Young Life volunteer and took a teaching job in a Christian prep school in Dallas. Life was definitely taking more of a servant turn, but I tended to gravitate to the Blonde, sunshine-achieving students and felt awkward around those who struggled. On weekends I was still looking for the man of my dreams.

One weekend I went with a friend to a pool party and met his friend, a seminary student just back from a summer missions trip. We laughed at Haiti tales and college tales, and, to my date's disappointment, something clicked between his friend and me.

The next weekend I went to Austin for an alumni outing where I reconnected with a fellow I'd known from a distance as president of the student body my freshman year. We both remained in the hill country an extra day because . . . something clicked.

The two dating relationships unfolded like a script. So often we only glimpse the larger significance of our lives in hindsight as we see the whole picture outside any given scene. Only then can we trace God's hand or have a sense of what he was up to. But each week that I continued to date the seminary student and the lawyer, the plotline became more evident. I was keenly aware of the choice shaping up.

It would be hard to say which one was taller, more handsome, or had a drier sense of humor, and both were brilliant. A typical evening with the seminary student was a bucket of chicken, him working on his studies while I wrote lesson plans. There was no typical date with my lawyer friend. Some weekends it was university football with official receptions. Others it was tennis at the club and dinner with friends. My little Blonde heart loved the jets and the Jaguar.

On the same weekend one told me he loved me, and the other asked me to marry him. For weeks I lived in indecision, very aware that this was a defining choice: Cosmic Blonde Tap Dancer vs. Servant. For life. It wasn't just that one was a rising trial lawyer with bright political prospects and the other was in ministry. Ministry would mean going to the mission field. That was part of the offer on the table.

When we are raising our kids to love God and love what he loves, we can never know how or when the values we build into their lives will make a difference. But we can never underestimate the importance of a godly heritage. I knew that life with Jack would have God at the center. As much as I enjoyed the parties, dinners, museums, resorts, and deep conversations with my lawyer friend, there were many times I felt a few steps off-center. It's not that he wasn't a Christian, but he didn't have the vision for God and his kingdom that Jack did. As I stood at that great crossroads into my future, I could not walk away from my past.

Something more was in play. Something I think is an even greater struggle among singles trying to choose their mates today. I had such high expectations of Prince Charming. I loved Jack's energy and passion for truth and life. If only I could have taken my scissors and trimmed away Jack's vision and pasted him into my lawyer friend's dreams and lifestyle. The mission field was Jack's vision, not mine. I considered going because of my vision for relationship, home, and family. Perhaps my missionary vision was clouded by war stories from Thailand. Of knowing firsthand what it was like to have to send your children off to a mission school. Of seeing my great aunt and uncle suffer from what seemed like more than their share of trauma and disease.

We can have such high expectations, such enchanted worldly visions of Happily Ever After that we miss Prince Charming. We peruse the good and perfect gifts God is holding out on a platter and look back at the horizon waiting for . . . what? And the enemy smirks, savoring his ability to ratchet our expectations so high that we are constantly scanning the horizon of fantasy, unable to open our hearts with gratitude to God's gift of reality in plain sight.

Looking back on it, Jack, the seminary student, says, "Well, the choice was really easy. Did I want to live life as an affluent celebrity or obey God, marry him, and take a vow of poverty?"

Choosing Jack was another step out of and away from my small story. Like Ruth, I followed my husband to a career in theological education in Central America. Although to say "like Ruth" gives me way more credit than was due. I was more reluctant than Ruth. I was the only somewhat-reformed Cosmic Blonde Missionary I knew. Even after we were married, I didn't wholeheartedly absorb his vision to be an educator in a country where biblical training was desperately needed. Mixed in with my fear and disappointment at the prospect of giving up my good-life dreams was another factor: My vision for ministry had been growing in a different direction.

My last year in Austin my mom had introduced me to Christian apologist Francis Schaeffer. Reading his books, I began to reflect more critically upon my Cosmic Blonde tap-dancing soul. I discovered worldview, the big picture of *How Should We Then Live?*—a Christian understanding of the way the world works and the "rise and decline of Western thought and culture." It was like finding the missing frame of a puzzle. A much larger portion of that vision of life came into focus. I felt as if I had spent three years in college trick-or-treating at all the different departments and had a nice sack of goodies, but studying worldview helped me understand how what I learned in different subject areas all flowed from our historical acceptance or rejection of God's truth and how all the different subjects fit together. (Except math. To me, math never fit with anything.)

My discovery had been like the scene in *Camelot* where King Arthur meets rusty, old King Pelinore, who prophetically mentions Arthur's "round table." Overjoyed, Arthur realizes he has stumbled upon his destiny. The more I studied worldview, the more I felt that I had discovered the thing for which I was made. I am a Big Picture person, but no one had been able to pierce my Blondeness with the Big Picture before.

Inspired by Schaeffer, I had begun teaching a course on Christian worldview at our high school and enrolled in a master's program in teaching the humanities at the University of Texas at Dallas. My old intellectual appetite had returned with a vengeance. Summers and nights I had feasted at the banquet of the History of Ideas and Aesthetics—never getting enough of art history, courses in the Renaissance, the Reformation, Islam—and I had delighted in passing on what I was learning to my students. Going to the mission field seemed like using my notebooks on non-objective art to build a campfire to roast lizard.

Our first step toward a formal commitment was to spend a summer in Preliminary Missionary Training. One night I was hanging in a hammock between two trees in the lost jungles of southern Mexico. Beyond civilization, beyond roads, beyond the mission airstrip, beyond even the meager creature comforts of the Wycliffe base camp. Squeezed between two walls of torrential rain falling on either side of my elbows, I was trying to keep so still that I wouldn't give my plastic hammock cover the slightest excuse to leak. Between showers the strange sonar bugs would ping each other, and the frogs had drunken puddle orgies. Against the dissonance of the jungle soundtrack, the plasma screen of my imagination ran pictures of luminous Italian Renaissance frescoes and delicate Dutch interiors. Michelangelo. Massaccio. Vermeer. Holbein. *Now, why am I doing this?*

Soft snores from Jack's hammock joined the pings and croaks. The link from my world to the other hammock seemed so fragile. *Lord, thank you that I don't have to be a real missionary. Thank you that we're going to the city, not the jungle. Father, for the first time I feel like I have found the vision for ministry that makes my heart soar. I love worldview, love the big picture. I love art and history and thinking about how the world pushes in on us. I love helping these kids push back. But there's this other dream—to go where he goes . . . and what happens to Michelangelo?*

We made our commitment and raised our financial and prayer support. The day came when we loaded up my parents' old Suburban and headed south for language school in Costa Rica. An emotional divide ran through the front seat. Jack's joy ran down to the Atlantic. He could not have been more excited to begin his life's big adventure. My tears flowed toward the Pacific. I wept for the loss of my parents and friends, the house in the nice neighborhood, and all my tap-dancing dreams. Even my newer kingdom dreams of teaching worldview.

And how did God reward my great sacrifice?

Even before we left for Costa Rica, my feet were becoming sore. The doctor thought it was probably post-snow-skiing trauma, and he prescribed anti-inflamatants. On our two-week journey south the soreness crept into my knees and my hips. I wondered if the tension of driving eight-hour days along highway lanes three feet wide with 600-foot dropoffs and through potholes the size of a hot tub was making me ache.

Two weeks after we arrived in Costa Rica, I was diagnosed with rheumatoid arthritis.

3

"LIKE THAT'S GONNA HAPPEN"

"You were expecting Prince Charming?"
SHREK

My descent from slightly tarnished Beauty Queen to cripple was swift. I felt like Snow White stuck in the body of the hobbling hag with the poisoned apple. Even my Snow Whiteness was anemia-induced. All my dreams leaked out of my heart and left a barren grief that occasionally trickled down my cheeks as I passed certain sign-posts—the days I could no longer play my guitar or wear my wedding ring—the little swollen, aching things that stood for the big broken thing. What happens to your dreams of performance when you can't even mount the steps to the stage?

Fatigue was a constant companion, but I dreaded going to bed. Freed from attending to the distractions of the day, my brain could only focus on the pain invading yet another joint. The disease that first attacked my feet, then my knees and hips, marched slowly up my body. The weight of the bed sheet on my toes felt like the lead X-ray vest they tuck around you at the dentist's. I would want to turn on my side for relief, but to push on my swollen elbows and shoulders and hips to make it happen was like choosing a brief flogging. The night my jaw joint began to ache, I stared into the darkness: *Surely, this must be it. Thank you, Jesus, that there are no joints farther up-line in my brain.* However, the pain in the already affected joints so weakened me that I couldn't stand up from a chair without help. My walking slowed to a shuffle.

I spiraled into a black hole of pain and loss. I knew that nothing penetrated God's protective hedge around my life except by his permission. I knew that he would work all the pain into something good. I knew, I knew, I knew all the things I had written in my Bible study notebooks about suffering, but I began to take the real measure of a divided heart. I never imagined a God who loved me so passionately that he would *not* let me settle for such a small love for him.

I knew God from a distance. But I couldn't see the distance. I never thought to compare the intensity of my desire for him to the way I had cruised by my high school boyfriend's house, hoping to catch a glimpse of his smile. Nor the way I had torn open a letter from my best friend when she moved to Hawaii. Nor the way I loved having Jack's arms around me. I truly thought I was loving God the way I was supposed to. I never deeply considered *what it meant to him* for me to approach him so casually, more often out of duty or desperation rather than delight. To open his Word more to answer Bible study questions than to seek and savor his company. My prayers were long on lists, short on the same eagerness and joy that I shared with friends.

I cried out to God across the distance, and I know he heard me. Within two weeks of being diagnosed with rheumatoid arthritis, I became pregnant—God's sweet gift of mercy in a dark, painful place. But my pregnancy complicated my medical needs. My Costa Rican doctor wanted to shoot me full of steroids. My doctor back in Dallas rose up in full AMA indignation and cried, "Don't do it. Don't do it!" Only eight weeks after I arrived in Costa Rica, Jack and I decided I should return to Texas for consultations with my doctors there while he continued with his course work.

So much of happiness rides not on where we really are in the moment, but where we expect to be. I live in the future—so much so that on one vacation my friends presented me with an award in recog-

nition of my relentless field marshal need to have a plan for the day—
the "What are we going to do next?" award.

I now had absolutely no idea what I was going to do next. My pictures of the future and the stage and all my Blonde tap-dancing dreams
faded to gray. In the airport with Jack, a giant question mark loomed
over our farewell. I didn't know when or if I would be returning to
Costa Rica or missions of any kind. I didn't know if I would have the
strength to mother our child or ever teach again.

We didn't know what the doctors would say. We didn't know if our
baby would suffer from my worsening illness. We didn't even know
when we would see each other again. I boarded the plane and collapsed
my aching body into my seat, fighting back tears and mostly winning,
until I saw Jack. Somehow he had found a place to park by the end of
the runway. As our plane roared past, he stood at the airport fence, waving and waving and blowing kisses.

I think I wept all over Nicaragua and maybe even Honduras. To my
pain, my cracked self-image, my broken dreams, and raging first trimester
hormones was added a profound sense of aloneness. Just when I needed
Jack the most, I was putting six hundred miles an hour between us.

Before I departed, a missionary friend had transferred from bus to
bus all the way across San Jose to bid me farewell and give me Chuck
Swindoll's little booklet *For Those Who Hurt*. When my sobs quieted, I
began reading the message taken from 2 Corinthians 1:1-3:

> *Praise be to the God and Father of our Lord Jesus Christ, the Father of*
> *compassion and the God of all comfort, who comforts us in all our trou-*
> *bles, so that we can comfort those in any trouble with the comfort we*
> *ourselves have received from God. For just as the sufferings of Christ*
> *flow over into our lives, so also through Christ our comfort overflows.*

"A teardrop on earth summons the King of heaven," Swindoll
wrote. God's compassion and comfort flowed off the pages. His tears
seemed to mingle with my own. It was as if he gathered all my swollen,
flaming joints and my numbed Blonde heart in his arms and loved me
deeply in the moment. I could never at that time have imagined sharing my story like this, but if you are reading this in a place of pain and
suffering, let me comfort you with the comfort God poured into my

throbbing soul that day. Even in our doubts and grief, even with a divided heart and a history of taking him for granted and focusing our passion elsewhere, God longs to enfold us in his love that surpasses all the knowledge in our heads and the notes in our notebooks.

Loath to turn my medical care back over to the steroid-happy doctor back in Costa Rica, my Dallas doctor recommended that I complete my "at risk" pregnancy in the States. In hopes we would return after the baby was born, Jack finished his courses and then packed our belongings and headed back to Texas. In the next scene of our bad missionary soap opera, a hurricane washed away the Pan American Highway in southern Mexico, leaving him to battle his own despair and dangerous mountain roads. He had blown his kisses on the runway in July. When he finally returned, it was October. We were invited to an associate pastorate at our home church where we would await our son's arrival and reevaluate my health and our future.

Dragging our U-Haul and our tails behind us, we arrived back in our Dallas area community late one night and fell into bed in a friend's guestroom. As usual, no matter what the personal pain or world crisis, Jack was asleep in four minutes flat. I lay there in the dark, feeling the jagged edges of my shattered dreams, groping around the void where my life was supposed to be, knowing in my head God was there but not feeling the covering of his "feathers" or the sense of his presence. The room was black and silent.

Like many other bereavements, loss of health becomes a journey of grieving. At the outset you can't absorb or imagine all the implications of the diagnosis. The realizations of loss and limitation flash unbidden on the screen of your imagination in the middle of doing dishes or driving to the store. One moment I was watching the autumn scenery slip by; the next I was looking for Kleenex and realizing, *I will never run with my child. I will never sit on the floor and play with him.*

The graces of friendship surrounded us, and the arrival of our healthy baby boy thrust us into new-parent hyperdrive—that combination of pride and joy and no sleep that carries you for a few weeks until the new normal sets in. But even with medications that reduced the pain and swelling, my illness vaporized dreams of the mission field.

Eventually we found ourselves in a small Bible institute ministry. In an economic downturn, sometimes we didn't get paid.

Studying worldview, I had learned that in God we find the answers to the biggest questions of life: How do we know what's true and right? Where have we come from? Where are we going? What are we supposed to be doing in the meantime? I discovered that you can know all this in your head—study it, teach it, apply it—and although your vision expands and life works on a certain level, your heart can surprise you. When the pressure and pain is unrelenting, it just may not want everything your head wants.

I also discovered that it is possible to do church, I mean really do church—Sundays, small group, women's Bible study, direct the choir, plan the special events—and still miss the thrill of worship and the comfort of God's intimate presence. All my life I'd been taught that if you have a passion for the truth of God's Word, everything will work out. If you just learn the facts, then the feelings will follow. And they did, but not in proportion to my desire for my Blonde Tap-Dancing dreams or to my pain when they shattered.

Without a vision of God that satisfies our longing for joy, without faith that what he promises to give us will delight us to the core, our hearts chase the promise of the next Golden Opportunity waiting just around the corner—new life, new love, new children, new career, new, new, new . . . If one image of future delight fades on the screen of our imaginations, we can change the channel. But sometimes we find ourselves in a place of final loss where we can't shop around for replacement parts for a broken life.

In the anti-fairy tale *Shrek*, the hero is an ogre. Ugly and crude with a bad attitude, he lives alone in a swamp and delights in mud baths, flatulence, and scaring the daylights out of the local townsfolk.

When Shrek rescues the princess, she asks, "Isn't this supposed to be a romantic moment?"

"Sorry, Lady, there isn't time."

"You're an ogre!"

"You were expecting Prince Charming?"

The princess is almost as crude as Shrek, eating roasted rats and attacking Robin Hood's merry men with Tai Kwan Do. At the big moment when Shrek finally kisses her, she is transformed . . . into an ogre as well.

As the spell breaks, all the beautiful stained-glass windows on the church explode. In case you miss the symbolism that these characters don't really need what a church has to offer, Shrek's dragon friend eyes the one remaining window and gives it a nice poke with his elbow. The ugly pair returns to the swamp to party with their friends in a nonstop knock-off of popular romantic songs.

And it's smart and hip and funny.

You want fairy tale dreams of love, beauty, truth, adventure? "Ha!" says Shrek. "Like that's gonna happen!" The best you can do in the real world is settle for far less. Give up on big dreams, high purpose.

One character in a story I read said, "Expectations are resentments waiting to happen." A woman quoted in an article on forgiveness said, "There is no such thing as forgiveness. I just lower my expectation of people."

Is *that* the answer to our broken dreams—to drastically lower the bar? To just settle for far less life than we dream of?

Some people do give up on their dreams and slide into a swamp of cynicism tinged with despair. They don't expect situations to improve or people to change. They don't expect to grab hold of the things they think will make them happy, and they don't expect that God can renew or transform their desires. On paper they may believe it, but they live like Shrek at the movie's beginning, posting his Keep Out! signs, withdrawn emotionally or even physically into a swamp of loneliness.

Others may open their hearts to fun and friendship, like Shrek at the end of the movie. After their final kiss, Shrek and the Princess blow off the wedding, leave the church in shambles, and head off to the swamp to party ever after. Chase after anything "new under the sun" that somebody hasn't already sent over the Web or printed on a T-shirt. They mock romantic dreams and joke about ideals—experts at lobbing the witty one-liner grenade. Cynical but sunny. Wildly self-indulgent and perhaps, like Solomon and the retired long-time editor of *Playboy,* destined to "lose their chops" for everything new under the sun.

Some people just cannot give up on broken dreams. They gather up the pieces and look around for a place to put them.

As the gap widened between my dreams of what my life would be and the reality of what it was turning out to be, my eventual response to the pain was pretty much a big sigh and a commitment to do my duty. I loved my husband. Loved my family. I wanted to honor and follow Christ too much to be overtly disobedient. I had lived in friendship with his people and enjoyed the protective boundary of his commands too long for the swamp of hedonism to have any great appeal for me. Alcohol, drugs, illicit sex—the way-out-of-bounds addictions held no attraction. Just as well. The thought of trying to rock and shimmy with a limp isn't pretty.

I prayed St. Lael's prayer of resignation:

WHAT GOESERE?
Lord, I know I should be happy with my lot.
If this is what you want for me,
Then give me the grace to settle for it.
Amen.

And he did . . . sort of. I lived on the edge of contentment. I did not lose heart, but it began to wander off into fantasies of the life I longed for. We are so used to life lining up in plotlines of conflict that lead to a resolution, a victorious climax. We have surgery to fix what's broken. We find a new job. A new husband. But when pain goes on and on unresolved, and dreams are divorced from reality by irreconcilable differences, what then? If this is as good as it gets, I'm getting out. At least for a little while.

My small, die-hard, Blonde-at-Heart Tap Dancing story went underground into an alternate universe.

I'm not talking about just dwelling upon pictures of a better life. I'm a creative person. I could write fairly engaging stories in my head. Stories where I could still ride the sunbeams, rack up the successes, and receive the attention and appreciation I longed for. Stories where I cast myself as the lead and spent hours living adventures beyond my reach. I felt that I had all this sparkle and talent and intellectual ability that was sinking beneath the burden of a chronic disease and the routines of baby care and daily life.

To make things worse, I am not a baby person. I was not freed to admit this in the company of Christian women until years later when no less a role model than Christian author Cynthia Heald uttered those very words at a conference. Out loud. From the platform. In front of hundreds of Christian women. "I am not a baby person," she confessed and went on to say that the Lord gave her four of them and refined her greatly in the process.

As a young woman of childbearing age, I was surrounded by baby persons. While they didn't rhapsodize over dirty diapers, their lives were filled up to the brim with nurturing children. They were absorbed in it and didn't seem to have any points hanging out unconnected like I did. When their children reached school age, many decided to home-school. Others, whose kids were in public school, decided the house was way too quiet when their youngest entered first grade; so they had another baby to fill their arms and liven things up. And I loved sharing life with these women. But I could tell by the way they celebrated baby care that, by comparison, I was baby challenged.

I remember Mark Twain's line: "Once a child becomes an adolescent, put him in a wooden barrel and feed him through the knothole. When he reaches sixteen, plug the knothole." Actually I enjoyed high schoolers more than babies. A veteran high school teacher and Young Life leader, I couldn't wait until Zach could talk with me and think with me. We read books "together" from the time he could stay awake longer than it took to eat.

I owned a master's degree in the history of ideas. I loved reading and teaching but spent most of my limited energy caring for Jack and Zach. I wish I had understood then what I do now about the preciousness of caregiving. I wish someone had challenged me to put more creativity into it and keep reading, reminding me, "This season shall pass, and you may teach again." Instead, I floated a lot—settled into a regular routine of nighttime TV. I didn't think I was watching "too much." It was my well-deserved reward. *Just make it through dinner and clean-up, and you can collapse into your chair and let the throbbing pain ebb away.* From news at 5:30 to news at 10:00, and a little beyond if Johnny's guests looked interesting, at twenty to twenty-five hours a week, it added up to a part-time job.

At the time I would never have described myself as mildly depressed. I was still Blonde enough that as long as I had my family and friends to enjoy, social dates on our calendar, and lovely vacations with my parents, I managed to stay on my little footpath along the edge of the abyss. Always the good student, I read my Bible to answer my weekly study questions and prayed plenty of "help me" prayers.

There were seasons when my escapes would become more frequent, but no one noticed. They couldn't see the storyline I picked up where I had left off as I was driving, or waiting in line, or getting dressed, or when my head hit the pillow at night. The extra time I spent daydreaming in bed could easily be chalked up to my physical pain. When you are in pain, it's easy for others to excuse you and to excuse yourself. The bed, the couch, the remote control are your best friends. The line between the rest you need and the escape you want blurs.

For months and years at a time I would lay my fantasies down. After a long absence, the urge to escape into my stories would return, often at night before I fell asleep. The Blonde part of me liked to think I was indulging in a gray area of behavior, but I began to sense Jesus wagging his head at me. And when I would try to resist the impulse, refuse to take the cue or write the story, it was as if someone widened the screen of my imagination and turned up the volume. The story dragged me into it. Like a vampire that stalked me in the dark, the only way to hold it at bay was to lift up the cross—start praying or quoting all those verses that earned me my childhood crowns. Sometimes, though, I gave up the fight. The stories enveloped me like the vampire's black cloak, dragging me down into the coffin, sucking my energy for real life dry. And I couldn't seem to find the silver stake that would put an absolute end to them.

Back in the early eighties, in the days before e-mail, chat rooms, or virtual games, my list of acceptable Christian escapes from an often painful reality was topped by TV, fantasy, and sleep. So many more options are available today. And you don't have to suffer from broken dreams to feel the pull to go there.

4

Oiling Our Dream Machinery

Most men and women lead a life at the worst so painful,
at the best so monotonous, poor and limited that the urge to escape,
the longing to transcend themselves if only for a few moments,
is and has always been one of the principal appetites of the
soul . . . the urge to escape from selfhood and the environment is
in almost everyone almost all the time.
ALDOUS HUXLEY, *THE DOORS OF PERCEPTION*

Welcome to the Museum of the American Mind, to the Exhibition on Imagination in particular—a multimedia tour of our dream machines where you can scan an article, listen to a snippet of talk radio, read a quote, click around in someone's inbox, read their journal—discover how these machines connect the secret needs and longings of our hearts to the private pictures that blaze on the screens of our imaginations. We'll drop behind the eyes of a few characters Walter Mitty-style and feel the tension, the pull against real life and real relationships. And I invite you to answer these questions as you read: What are these people gaining? What are they missing? Can you see any red flags? Do you recognize anything like your own dream machines on display?

(Slightly adapted from the Chris Baker Show, KPRC, Houston, Texas, April 2004.)

Good afternoon. This is Chip Butler on KSKP, and if you're just joining us, we're talking about big bucks spent on bizarre hobbies. We got started last hour talking about this article in the paper on expanding the tennis courts at Gateway Park. Sounds like a great idea, except it's got all the Frisbee Golfers with their shorts in a wad because the expansion would take in their favorite area to play."

Chelsea smiled and punched the volume-up button on her steering wheel.

"Yeah, and the reporter quoted this guy who said he always carries around a bagful of twenty to thirty Frisbees in his car. I started adding up thirty Frisbees at $10-$20 a pop, made some comment about it, and the phone lines lit up with all these other yahoos telling me, "You think a few hundred dollars worth of Frisbees is something, let me tell you about 'pimping my car' and 'my Old West fantasy weekends' . . . and here we are. Mike, you're on the air."

"Hi, Chip. I spend big bucks on croquet."

"Croquet?"

"Yeah, last year I finished in the top ten at the National Croquet Championship."

"Did you win a big prize? Do you play for money?"

"Ah, well, mostly trophies. I've traveled a lot. Got trophies from a lot of different states. Takes a lot of money to do that much traveling."

"Sure."

"I've also got a $400 mallet with a graphite shaft—"

"Really? A graphite shaft on a croquet mallet?"

"Yeah, if you really—"

"Okay, well, best of luck, Mike."

Chelsea inched along the freeway, shaking her head.

"Carl, this is Chip Butler. Thanks for calling KSKP. So what's your gig?"

"Slot cars."

"Slot cars? That takes big bucks?"

"Yeah, well, the track runs about five dollars a section. The cars are about forty dollars each. Half-scale Formula One racers—Mercedes, the hot stuff. Then I've got controllers and a computer to count the laps and—"

"So where do you have this big layout set up?"

"In my living room."

"Your living room? What does your wife say about that?"

"My wife's not around anymore."

That figures. Finally the traffic was picking up. Chelsea accelerated and eased into the exit lane.

"My girlfriend likes it though."

"Oh, well, that's good. Thanks, Carl. Good-bye. Yyyeah, I can just hear my wife coming in and finding Formula One track all over her living room. *Her* living room. . . . Hi, is this Evan?"

"Hi, Chip."

"Hi, Evan. Thanks for calling KSKP."

"My hobby isn't all over the living room, but my wife still gives me grief about it."

"Oh, what's that?"

"Hunting."

"Hunting? Don't you put food on the table? Shouldn't she be grateful?"

"Well, I hunt waterfowl, and she figures it costs about $500 an ounce."

"Whoa, how much do you spend a year on hunting?"

"I guess by the time you count the lease and the camo gear and the dogs and the pumps and the four-wheelers and the ammo and the decoys and guns, I maybe spend $40,000 a year."

"That's *serious* hunting. How many guns do you have?"

"I don't know. Two safes full. I just bought a new shotgun—"

"Didn't you already have a shotgun?"

"Yeah."

"Why'd you buy another?"

Chelsea bumped the up-volume button again.

"Because I wanted it."

Chelsea laughed with the DJ and his guest. *Sounds just like Will.* She slowed to join the line of cars turning into her subdivision.

"Richard, you're on the air. What bizarre hobby do you spend big bucks on?"

"Jousting."

"Jousting? No kidding? Like with armor and everything?"

"Yes."

"How much does a suit of armor cost?"

"Oh, anywhere from $3,000 to 5,000."

"Are they the same as what Lancelot wore?"

"They're historically accurate, but when you're looking at a collision at forty mph with a one-and-a-half-inch dowel rod, uh, we opt for modern padding."

"Sounds a little risky, Richard."

"Yeah, but the ladies, they like it. Ladies are really attracted to jousting."

"Oh, I'll bet—the 'simple joys of maidenhood.' Thanks for calling,

Richard. Do we have time for one more? One more before the break. . . .
Hello, Andy, we've got time for one more. What's your—"

"I've spent $25,000 on a Kiss tribute band."

"Holy moley!"

Chelsea burst out laughing as she pulled her car into the garage. She
turned the key off but kept listening to the radio.

"So you dress up in leather and paint your faces and . . ."

"And went out and played Kiss songs for parties and things. Spent
$2,000 on a Gene Simmons costume."

"How do you spend—"

"Custom leather. And I've got a $3,000 red axe bass."

"Are you good?"

"Oh, yeah, the fans loved us."

"Really? Cause if you're good—"

"We're great. *Were* great. We don't play too much now. Got all my stuff
in a storage locker."

"You gonna sell it?"

"I don't know. We might play again. I look back on it now and think,
What the hmmmm was I doing?"[4]

Chelsea opened the car door and nodded in agreement. *What* were *you
doing?* Inside the mailbox she smiled to see her new copy of *World* magazine, *Imprimis* from Hillsdale College, and a *National Review*. On the way to
the bedroom, she dropped the mail beside her end of the couch. She was
sprinkling two chicken breasts with her brother-in-law's special seasoning
when Will walked in.

"Hi, sweetheart." He pecked her on the cheek. "How was your
day?"

"Fine. Were you listening to Chip Butler's show on the way
home?"

"Yeah, could you believe it?" He grabbed the grill lighter and opened
the door to the deck. "Those guys are nuts."

When he came back in, Chelsea arched her eyebrow and shot him a
grin. "Did you notice they were all guys?"

"Hey, back off now!" He grinned in return. "They're just trying to even
the score with their wives' credit card bills. You women spend all these big
bucks at the mall, but the trouble is, nobody thinks it's bizarre."

"Very funny," she called after him as he headed to the bedroom to
change.

After dinner Chelsea stood at the back door watching the raindrops
spatter on the deck. "Too bad. I hoped we could take a walk."

"Yeah, too bad." Will lost no time pulling out his wireless laptop
and easing into his overstuffed chair. A few clicks later, he perused

the stats for his fantasy football team while the Raiders and the Vikings lit up the TV screen. He looked up and noticed her watching him from her spot on the couch. "Hey, aren't you glad my hobby is so normal? And cheap?"

She turned her gaze to the TV. "You have to watch it in here?"

"You want to turn on the news channel, don't you?"

Chelsea turned back to him but didn't respond.

"The thing is, Chels, you can watch the news on the smaller screen in the bedroom, and what will you miss? The laugh lines on the talking heads? But you can see the game so much better out here. Follow the action. I mean, that's one of the main reasons we bought this big TV, right?"

Chelsea shrugged and gathered up her mail. "You watched a game in here last night."

"Ah, the glory of ESPN." He searched her face to see how serious she was.

Finally she leaned down and kissed him. "Enjoy your game." She headed toward the bedroom.

At 10:30 Will came in and turned back the covers on the bed. "Vikings won."

She looked up at him from the sitting area. "Is that a good thing?"

"Yes, because my receiver, Randy Moss, made five catches, one for the winning touchdown."

"Randy Moss!" Chelsea rolled her eyes but then smiled. "Congratulations. Will it bother you if I watch *Nightline*?"

It was her turn to look over and see him watching her as he took off his socks. He stood up, dumped his socks in the hamper, and walked over to her chair in the sitting area. "Tomorrow night let's go visit parents. Which ones?"

"Ummm, sorry. Tomorrow is first Wednesday."

"Oh, that's right. And the election is coming up. I'm glad your hobby is normal and cheap too. Except for the conventions." He kissed her lightly on the head. Her gaze followed him into the bathroom and lingered on the door. When he emerged, she asked him again, "Will it bother you if I watch *Nightline*?"

He slid between the covers. "You won't keep me awake if that's what you mean." Reaching over, he turned off the bedside lamp. "Enjoy your show, Chels."

Chelsea turned back to the TV. The man was losing another loan to DiTech. She glanced toward the bed for a few moments and dropped her gaze back to her *World* magazine.

(Quoted from *The Houston Chronicle*, April 27, 2004)

Hugh Grant says he would agree to settle down and start a family only if he were utterly bored or drunk, reports Annanova.com. "When it gets to the point where I'm bored with myself, I'll start a family," Grant said. Grant does have specific plans for retirement: trading nightclubs for golf clubs. "I'm already to the point where I can't think of anything else. I used to read books on all kinds of topics, but now I only read about golf. It's turning me into a much more superficial person. Not that I used to be especially deep."

From: Lisa Rafferty
To: David Randolph

Hi, Coach!
Bon voyage to Lexington. You & the boys have worked so hard this year, and we are so proud we are obnoxious. I can't imagine a more exciting road to the playoffs. If you need inspiration, just turn around, and the entire Eng/Journ dept will blow kisses your way.

_____

From: David Randolph
To: Lisa Rafferty

Thanks, Lisa. I'll look for the kisses, but don't let Barbara see. I'm in enough trouble for spending every nite for 3 weeks straight at the gym. Thanks for the support.

Janice turned off the faucet and closed the dishwasher. Silence settled over the room, as piercing as when she had stepped in the door two hours ago. She picked up her glass and drank the last of the water.

Over the rim her eyes rested on the freshly turned earth of Missy's little grave out by the garage. She would have to get past the idea of "shopping for a replacement." To come home to this silence enlarged all the loneliness she thought she had lived down to a manageable size.

Thoughts of Missy took her back to the courtroom and watching Sam walk out. Back to the driveway the day after Christmas and watching Ethan drive off to his new job in Kansas City. At least *he* had given her a tender good-bye. But he didn't call to say hello very often. She sometimes had thoughts of following him there, but she didn't really think that being in the same town would close the distance between them. Besides, her friends and her church were here.

Although not *here* at the end of the day.

She turned on the dishwasher, glad for the hum and muffled spray, and looked at the clock. 7:45. Better than she thought. Only fifteen minutes. As she walked past the back door, her eyes took in Missy's scratches.

In the bedroom she picked up her phone message notes and thought about calling Cindy. But she knew she couldn't count on just a fifteen-minute call. Better to call tomorrow. She stared again at the second message: "Friends Helping Friends—7:30." She should have gone. Maybe this new ministry to women in transition would open a door out of the silence. She had certainly logged a few transitions of her own. But at the price of having to talk about Sam or finding a rental house or a job or a lawnmower or insurance or a thousand other things she had lost in that courtroom? There were harder things than silence.

She sat down at her desk and thought about calling Ethan. That would certainly take less than fifteen minutes. But she had just called him Sunday. She looked at her "not so urgent" pile of papers: the Compassion envelope waiting for a check and a short message to Marisela in Honduras, the extra copies of their Christmas photos and scrapbooking stickers she wanted to put in the little album she'd bought to send her sister, a wedding invitation, a birthday card for her niece, letters to answer, a few articles she'd clipped and wanted to pass along, other papers laid in the stack so long ago she no longer recognized them. She could pull out her note cards or find the little photo album. She could sort through her pile and get rid of all the things she had hoped to get to but were now over three months past the meaningful window of doing them.

The clock on her computer screen read 7:57, but it ran four minutes fast. She scrolled down her inbox of unopened messages, mostly from Internet friends. She thought about the days when she would come home and spend the entire evening in chat rooms and answering e-mail. Somehow the excitement of meeting scrapbookers in Seattle and Phoenix didn't draw her into the cyber circle like it used to. As she clicked the mouse to log off, she noticed that her manicure was fading around the edges. From the bathroom cabinet she collected her nail care kit and deposited it on the ottoman in front of her chair. She turned on the TV and went to the kitchen. From the pantry she pulled out a bag of Newman's Own and put it in the microwave.

At 8:00 sharp the movie channel's familiar theme song summoned her to the living room. Janice nestled into her chair. She shouldn't really feel this much pleasure over warm, fake buttery popcorn and old black and white movies. Her eyes closed to savor the kiss of the music and the fresh-popped fragrance of Paul Newman.

(Quoted from the *New York Times*, August 1998)

Study Examines Health of Web Users

Researchers at Carnegie Mellon University have found that people who spend even a few hours a week online experience higher levels of depression and loneliness than they would have if they used the computer network less frequently. . . . Research on the effects of watching television indicates that it tends to reduce social involvement. But the new study, titled "HomeNet," suggests that the interactive medium may be no more socially healthy than older mass media.

Researchers hypothesize that relationships maintained over long distances without face-to-face contact ultimately do not provide the kind of support and reciprocity that typically contribute to a sense of psychological security and happiness, like being able to baby-sit in a pinch for a friend or to be able to grab a cup of coffee. . . . "Our hypothesis is there are more cases where you're building shallow relationships, leading to an overall decline in feelings of connection to other people."

"It's not clear what the underlying psychological explanation is," Bikson (a senior scientist at the Rand research institute) said of the study. "Is it because people give up day-to-day contact and then find themselves depressed? Or are they exposed to the broader world of the Internet and then wonder, 'What am I doing here in Pittsburgh?'"

From: Lisa Rafferty
To: David Randolph

Hi, Coach:
Well, how does it feel to be in the finals? We could not believe your last down-to-the-buzzer play! :>o They never expected Dexter, but the boy came through. We almost mobbed you, but saw Barbara and thought better of it. Maybe we need to give you a private mobbing in the faculty lounge.

_____

From: David Randolph
To: Lisa Rafferty

You can give me a private mobbing any time.

_____

From: Lisa Rafferty
To: David Randolph

Can we settle for sharing a table at lunch tomorrow? You can give me your input on the photo spread of the game for this week's BANNER. We snapped some great pix of you in serious diplomatic negotiations with the ref.

A good day ain't got no pain.
On a bad day I just lie in bed
and think of things that might have been.

SIMON AND GARFUNKLE, "SLIP-SLIDIN' AWAY"

I'm looking out the peephole into the hallway. No, not an apartment. I'm looking out the back door of my place in Rancho Bernardo. No, the front window of my condo in . . . Newport Beach. Yes, Newport. Beyond my driveway the hillside drops away to the coast, and Catalina slumbers offshore in a magic purple mist. I see Brad's car turn into my driveway.

I look in the mirror and smooth my hair, tucking the blonde streaks behind my ears. With little diamond studs. I'm finally down to a size six, and it feels so good. That tight, hungry feeling.

I watch Brad roll out of his Porsche. All tan and white teeth and, oh, I forgot how good the guy looks. He's carrying . . . mmm, he remembers . . . pink stargazer lilies. He walks toward the front door with that smooth glide. He was always so smooth, like a Bond star. A little more Brosnan and Moore than Connery. More dash than grit.

He looks . . . tenuous. Second thoughts? *You're the one who started the e-mails and asked for dinner.*

He rings the bell.

"Hi, Amy." His face lights up the California sunshine.

"Hi, Brad."

He looks at me like he's scanning every detail and sending it to memory. "Wow. You look just as beautiful as always. No, even more so." He hands me the lilies.

I laugh and feel the tingle of embarrassment and heat. "Thanks. You remembered—"

"I remember everything. I remember how you used to drive me crazy just walking into American History. I remember how you used to sit by the window and show a lot more interest in the blue sky than Prof. Sander's lectures. I remember it took a good six weeks to get you looking my way."

"Not true. I spent six weeks staring out the window imagining what it would be like to go out with you."

His smile faded. He ran his hand through his hair, and the hesitancy returned. "Amy, I was . . . I was going to wait . . ."

Brad doesn't do awkward. But all the smooth has disappeared.

"I hadn't planned to get into this right away. But seeing you . . ." Brad catches both my hands and holds them tightly. "Amy, I can't believe I ever let you go. I got distracted by all the rush up the ladder and the shorter skirts. Let the press go to my head. You finally get your hands on all this sparkle and glitter out there, and then . . . it's like . . . stumbling backstage at Disneyland. You realize it's all paste and rhinestones and Velcro and a well-oiled machine that moves dreams down the conveyor belt like the little cars in the Haunted Mansion."

I can't believe these words are tumbling out of his mouth, words I would have given my degree, my job offers, and my very soul to have heard three years ago. I want to say, *I forgive you*, but now opened, the old wounds need more balm.

"I understood the shorter skirts, Brad, but I have never understood Robin. When you were ready to take life seriously, you didn't come back to me." The tears I thought I had stopped crying a long time ago pool barely below the surface.

Brad looks away for a long time and then back to me. "You always wanted so much from me, Amy. You always wanted to go deep, take risks. You wanted me to meet you in a place that was so much work to get to. I just wanted to relax. I thought, *Life is hard. Relationships shouldn't be something you have to work at.* I was graduating, launching into real life. I wanted to work hard and get together for dinner and a movie, enjoy friends on weekends, and church on Sunday. That's all Robin wanted."

I close my eyes and think of the times I woke up on the couch at 2:00 A.M., surrounded by damp Kleenex. "Is that supposed to be a consolation?" I can't help the edge in my voice. He catches it. I definitely nicked him, and he's smarting. With great effort I dab a little tenderness on the cut.

"I'm sorry, Brad." I let the anger out in a big sigh. "So what happened?"

"It . . . it wasn't . . . enough. About a year, and I knew it. It took another six months to tell her. And then . . . it's taken me a while to get my courage up." He looks so painfully hopeful. Like a child without quite enough money at the ice cream truck.

"It only took six weeks the first time."

"That's because all I wanted to do the first time was ask you out."

I search his face. His eyes surprise me with an intensity and depth I can't remember seeing before. "And this time?"

He pulls my arms around his waist, and his arms encircle me. "This time I knew if I jumped back in, it would be in the deep end. Amy, I've missed you."

I hear the front door open. "Amy, I'm home." The condo in Newport vaporizes into the reality of our tract home in La Mirada. I jump up and straighten the bed and duck into the bathroom. After a Q-tip for my smudged mascara and a few whisks of the brush, I grab the trashcan and find Colin in the kitchen, rummaging the depleted pantry shelves.

"Hi, Colin." I kiss him on the cheek and escape to the laundry room where I empty the bathroom trash into the larger can and the washer into the dryer. Colin appears in profile at the door, one eye on my sudden blur of activity. He throws his head back, coaxing the last few sunflower seeds out of a sack, and then wads it up and pitches it into the trash.

"How was your day?"

"Fine. I have an interview with Whittington and Preston on Friday."

"That's great, Amy. You know, if you need me to go shopping, I'll be glad to help."

The poor guy is starving, and a trip to the store will be the quickest way to put his hands on some food. "I'm sorry, honey." I walk to the kitchen desk and tear off the shopping list that has been hanging there for three days. "I meant to get this done today."

He looks it over and then looks back at me.

Say something, Colin. Come after me. Put it all together—

Colin circles his arms around me and gives me a long kiss. He drops his forehead onto mine and smiles. "I'll be glad when you find a new job. You are *totally* off your rhythm." He gives me another squeeze. "I'll take my cell. Call if you think of anything else."

I listen to his car pull away. *I could go after him. Wade into the mine-field. I could ask him if he really needs more than a full pantry and clean jeans. And if he doesn't?* I slump down on the bed.

Brad walks me down the Newport boardwalk. Past the trampo-lines full of chubby non-athletes who turn leg-waving flips in the safety harnesses, giggling with delight. Past the Popeyed young men who never tire of sledge-hammering the bell-ringer that measures their manhood and the Olive Oiled women who never tire of admir-ing their muscles.

We park at the rail overlooking the mega-millions floating in the Newport marina, and Brad pulls me close beside him. "Amy, I know you're in a hard place. But you couldn't work under a man who stole all the credit for your team's success. And your promo-tion. Tell me how you're feeling. Now that you've ridden that wave of justifiable anger all the way to the beach, is that how you feel . . . beached?"

"Yes. Stranded, alone. Like a big soggy overweight blob of com-plete inertia."

"Amy," Brad turned and took my chin in his hand, "you are a daz-zling package of marketing savvy and creative energy. You are The Baxter Group's loss and Whittington and Preston's gain. If they don't snap you up . . ."

> *The mind . . . is the place of our widest and most basic freedom. Of all the things we do, we have more freedom with respect to what we will think of, where we will place our mind than anything else. . . . We sim-ply turn our mind to whatever it is we choose to think of. The deepest revelation of our character is what we choose to dwell on in thought—as well as what we can or cannot even think of.*
> DALLAS WILLARD, *THE DIVINE CONSPIRACY*

> *Finally, brothers, whatever is true . . . think about such things.*
> PAUL, APOSTLE OF JESUS CHRIST (PHIL. 4:8)

From: Lisa Rafferty
To: David Randolph

Well, just 2 more days. Trying to teach anything but sports journ right now is like flipping over to PBS in the middle of the Super Bowl. I don't know how you can stand it. Even if you win, it's sad to think that next week our joyride will be over.

_____

From: David Randolph
To: Lisa Rafferty

Yes, but then I'll actually have a life. I may not have a wife, but I'll have a life.

_____

From: Lisa Rafferty
To: David Randolph

David, are you serious?

_____

From: David Randolph
To: Lisa Rafferty

Yes. She's packing. But not for the finals. As always, impeccable timing.

_____

From: Lisa Rafferty
To: David Randolph

David, I'm so sorry. I'm trying not to think unchristian thoughts about Barbara, but . . . keep your eyes on the stands. An entire school loves and supports you. An entire community. I talk with the kids and know how much they adore you. You are not only the greatest coach Stratton has ever had, but you are a man our boys want to be like. I want my boy to be like.

❦

(Adapted freely from "Suburban Rhapsody," *Psychology Today*, November/December 2003)

VIRTUAL OBSESSION

Local Woman Knew She Was in Trouble When a Social Worker Knocked on Her Door

Halfway through her first pregnancy, local personal trainer Caroline Thompson decided to take a high-tech approach to parenthood. She bought a copy of The Sims, the hugely popular computer game that lets you create and direct a household and a family—building a suburban home, finding jobs for the parents and scrambling to keep everyone happy and healthy. She fired it up, selecting a young professional couple with a newborn. Hey, it was a game. How hard could it be?

Whoops. "You know what? The babies cry a lot in that game," she says. "So it's crying while I'm trying to juggle everything else, like getting the parents to work and making sure they clean the house." After a few hours of domestic chaos, her virtual baby was whisked away by a digital caseworker. "I was devastated! I was sure that I wouldn't be able to handle a real baby," Thompson says with a laugh. She kept playing though, and by the time baby Lilly arrived, she felt like a pro. "My family thought I was nuts, but I swear it got me through the pregnancy," she says.

Now Mom is having to adjust her playing habits. "I'll be playing along and hear Lilly waking up and think, *It can't have been two hours.* Now I'm addicted, and I tease Lilly, 'It's all your fault!' Usually she's happy enough in the playpen by the computer if I want to keep playing for a while. If not, I've discovered I can hold her and still play if I bring in the portable TV and position it so Lilly can watch *Teletubbies.*"

Thompson's next Sims assignment is learning what it will be like to add Lilly's little brother or sister. "I practice balancing Lilly in my lap and taking care of my Sims baby at the same time. Lilly is learning from it too. The other day my Sims Mom set the stove on fire and the baby started crying. I was panicked that the social worker might show up again; so without even thinking, I was trying to quiet my Sims baby: 'Oh, darlin', what's the matter? What's wrong?' Lilly looked up at me, expecting my attention. I had to tell her, 'Not you, Lilly.'"

❦

From: Lisa Rafferty
To: David Randolph

David, congratulations. You played your hearts out. No one has ever taken us as far. Words fail me. I'm so proud of our boys. Proud of you and all your staff. You held your heads high at the end, which you should have. It was just Westchester's year. We're planning a celebration anyway.

PS. Did Barbara really leave?

————————————

From: David Randolph
To: Lisa Rafferty

Lisa, I was hoping you'd be here in my inbox. Thank you and, yes, she did. It's the morning after. Spent all last night watching game films. Was afraid what might happen if I stopped. Want to share lunch again? Don't feel too public today but I'd like to talk. How about bringing your salad to my office? I could really use that private mobbing.

＊＊＊＊＊

> *. . . bringing into captivity every thought to the obedience of Christ.*
>
> PAUL THE APOSTLE (2 COR. 10:5)

September 5
Dear Lord:
Glossy mags. Dark theaters. Melanie's vacation pictures. The invitations on my computer screen. The enemy torches my dreams with ever-new images of lives I'll never live. I turn off the TV, but my heart still longs to escape into fantasy or my computer. All these options—you'd think I'd feel so free. But I feel so stuck. I want something so much more than my little life.

Have you been sending secret messages to Pastor Rob? I felt like he looked straight at me today when he said, "Commitment without vision = a life of Christian duty." That's me, Lord. Trying to do my duty. But with all the dream machines and virtual anything at my fingertips, duty doesn't hold me like it used to.

You've taken so many of my dreams, and mostly what's left in my imagination are the pictures from my books, my TV, and movies, and the plotlines I spin in my private moments. Are my fantasies so wrong? Is it wrong to dream of rescuing people or winning the lottery and giving the money away? I miss romance, Lord. Is it wrong to enjoy the thrill of being noticed and chosen and cherished again? What about my e-mail chats with Eric? Is that what they're about? Lord, you know I would never do anything.

When I escape to another world, another life in my head or my screens, what does it mean? Is all this free play of my imagination in fields of dreams as good as it gets?

Lord, why does seeing you, wanting you have to be so hard? I need a vision of you that is stronger than the delight of my distractions and fantasies, that grabs me more than images of the good life. How do I see the truth of who you are and the reality of your unseen kingdom? How does it become more real to me than this world I see every day? How does it grab my heart so that I want you " more than these"?

God show me . . . if you'd just SHOW ME! Like Pastor Rob said, I need a "vision of life" beyond boredom and fantasy and settling. How do you grow that kind of vision in my heart? Could you just show up? Suddenly? In all your Technicolor glory? You've done that with a few people . . .

5

CLOSE
ENCOUNTER

God is a mystery of such depth, power and beauty
that if we were to see (him) head on, in any way other than
glimpses, I suspect we should be annihilated.
PASTOR AND AUTHOR FREDERICK BUECHNER

In the early days of our marriage B.C. (Before Child), in the days when we traveled light without a diaper bag and three meals and four changes of clothes and a shelf full of toys and a Sassy Seat and a stroller, back in those days when we could just think and then charge, we went to see one of Steven Spielberg's early flights of imagination, *Close Encounters of the Third Kind.*

At the end of the movie I said to Jack, "Well, Moses went to the mountain, but he met aliens instead of God." Jack had noticed the same thing. We began listing the similarities between Moses' encounter with God and the close encounters with aliens in the movie, when one of the rolling credits stopped us cold: "*The Ten Commandments*, used by permission." For the first and last time in our lives we sat back down and watched the same movie, start to finish.

In the scene where Richard Dreyfus builds an alien-inspired massive replica of Devil's Tower mountain in his living room, we found it: *The Ten Commandments* was playing on the TV in the background, followed by the old Budweiser commercial singing, "Here comes the King; here comes the big number one . . ." And I thought, *It was no coincidence that* Close Encounters *was filmed when that movie and commercial were being broadcast.*

Spielberg was tipping his hat, borrowing his imagery right out of Exodus 19—the thunderous rumbling, trumpet sounds blaring, the dark clouds like smoke that covered the mountain, the descent of the starship as the people gathered below watching in awe, the scientists speaking to the alien ships in musical code and the alien ship answering back. It was a scene written long ago when God did the very thing we long for, the thing we think we want: He showed up, came near his people at Mount Sinai.

> On the morning of the third day there were thunders and lightnings and a thick cloud on the mountain and a very loud trumpet blast, so that all the people in the camp trembled. Then Moses brought the people out of the camp to meet God, and they took their stand at the foot of the mountain. Now Mount Sinai was wrapped in smoke because the Lord had descended on it in fire. The smoke of it went up like the smoke of a kiln, and the whole mountain trembled greatly. And as the sound of the trumpet grew louder and louder, Moses spoke, and God answered him in thunder.

In Spielberg's movie, the drama of the close alien encounter plays out on the faces of the number-crunching, left-brain scientists and battle-hardened warriors. Smitten with awe and wonder at what has never been seen by human eyes, they watch the twinkly, sleek little space ships doing their choreographed song and dance. Awe morphs into angst when the big mother ship finally slides around the mountain.

The same wonder mixed with jubilant anticipation shines from the faces of people in the movie *Independence Day* as they gather, not at the mountain, but on the top of the skyscraper to welcome the aliens to earth. Again the drama plays out on eagerly uplifted faces watching the hovering ship finally move to connect with earth. The spacecraft's bottom shield opens, displaying a beautiful light show. Laser beams converge into a massive beam of explosive energy. Smiles fade, jaws slack, eyes widen, the blood drains away. The beam incinerates the people and the skyscraper and the city in a fiery shockwave of alien power.

The last looks on their faces remind me of the faces of the damned in Michelangelo's *The Last Judgment*. Demons clutching their legs and dragging them down to hell, a hand shielding one eye, the other eye full of reckoning: *The thing I feared . . . is true.*

What words describe the shock on faces like that?

Jesus' words? "Woe, woe to you . . ."

Dante's words? "All hope abandon ye who enter here."

The lyric from one of my favorite movie soundtracks, *The Lion in Winter?* "*Media vita in morte sumus*—In the midst of life we are in death."

What would we feel in the presence of a living being completely "other" than ourselves? Awe? Wonder?

Perhaps it would depend upon the power of the being. What would we feel if we found ourselves utterly vulnerable in the presence of someone who has the power of being—the power to give or destroy life on the spot? Hope? Fear? Determination? Anxiety?

Maybe it would depend upon our sense of danger. What is the heart and intent behind the power? In *Close Encounters* the aliens came in peace. In *Independence Day* they came in war. When God showed himself to Moses and the people of Israel gathered at the foot of the mountain, did he come in peace or war? What did they feel? What did such a meeting mean to them?

The author of Hebrews tells us they came to a quaking mountain burning with fire and covered with darkness, gloom, and storm. A mountain that couldn't be touched on peril of death.

And they were terrified.

When they heard the trumpet blast and the voice speaking to them, they begged Moses, "Stop! Please, stop! We can't bear any more!" The sight was so terrifying that even Moses said, "I tremble with fear."

We so long to see God. But is that it? Is that who we would find if God were to show up suddenly in all his glory? A God so holy and powerful and threatening that we cringe in terror before him?

God's prophet Ezekiel saw "what looked like a throne of sapphire, and high above on the throne was a figure like that of a man. I saw that from what appeared to be his waist up he looked like glowing metal, and that from there down he looked like fire; and brilliant light surrounded him. Like the appearance of a rainbow in the clouds on a rainy day, so was the radiance around him" (Ezek. 1:26-28 NIV). Ezekiel saw God in his rainbow radiance, and when he saw it . . . he fell facedown.

Daniel saw a vision of the Ancient of Days taking his seat on his throne of "fiery flames; its wheels were burning fire. A stream of fire issued and came out from before him; a thousand thousands served him, and ten thousand times ten thousand stood before him; the court sat in judgment, and the books were opened" (Dan. 7:9-10). Daniel didn't drop, but he was "anxious" and so "alarmed" that all the color drained from his face.

When Peter, James, and John climbed the mountain with Jesus, he changed before their eyes. "His face shone like the sun," and "his clothes became radiant, intensely white, as no one on earth could bleach them." Moses and Elijah appeared, and Peter was so overwhelmed he began making up stupid things to say. I think Peter was a Cosmic Blonde. When God's voice spoke out of the bright cloud, the disciples "fell on their faces and were terrified."

John is with Ezekiel. He reports in Revelation 1 that he hears a voice, and when he turns and sees Jesus' resurrected face shining like the sun in all its brilliance, he "fell at his feet as though dead."

Our desire to see God in his glory brings us to this overwhelming person before whom godly people shrink and cringe and keel right over. *Is that the picture you want us to carry in our imaginations, God? Are you just too much for us?*

Behind and outside the story of life is one supremely important and constant reality: Before there ever was an "In the beginning . . . ," there was God on the throne.

I invite you to come with me, stand before him, face to face. This is a person, a place, and a picture that needs to blaze on the screen of our imaginations. It is the only reality in life that really matters when students are shot in school hallways and twin towers fall. We need to see God and see his heart. And we need to know what it means for us.

What would it be like to come before the Creator of the Universe in all his glory? Not in judgment, but just the everyday reality of God? According to the sixth chapter of Isaiah's book, God suddenly shows up to the prophet:

> *In the year that King Uzziah died, I saw the Lord sitting upon a throne, high and lifted up; and the train of his robe filled the temple. Above him stood the seraphim. Each had six wings: with two he covered his face, and with two he covered his feet, and with two he flew. And one called to another and said: "Holy, holy, holy is the LORD of hosts; the whole earth is full of his glory!" And the foundations of the thresholds shook at the voice of him who called, and the house was filled with smoke. (6:1-4)*

Can you smell the smoke and hear the seraph's crashing song? Isaiah is perhaps still mourning the loss of the king. In the wake of something close to a national catastrophe, the kingdom of heaven opens, and he sees God seated on his throne.

Imagine this temple in heaven, the real thing after which the earthly tabernacle and temple were patterned. The author of Hebrews tells us that the tabernacle "is a copy and shadow of what is in heaven" (NIV), and Moses was warned, "See that you make everything according to the pattern that was shown you on the mountain." The reality that is our world flows out of a heavenly reality more real than the chair in which I'm sitting or the trees outside my window. There was a throne in heaven before there was ever a throne on earth. Perhaps it's programmed into our system to have a certain awe and reverence for a just and righteous King seated on his throne.

Pastor and author Bill Hybels confirms what we know in our hearts: "People love to be well led." Something in our souls longs to line up behind leadership of passion and vision and truth. If we're too democratic to bow before a king, we'll anoint celebrities.

Maybe you've been to Europe and been in a real throne room. I have. The kings were long gone, but the vacant throne, beautifully carved and overlaid with gold, still stirred a sense of awe in my heart.

Isaiah doesn't tell us what God's throne looks like. Perhaps it is great and gleaming white, like the throne on which God will be seated at the last judgment. Perhaps it glitters with "the appearance of a sapphire" like the throne Ezekiel saw. I'm sure it is greater than Solomon's, and we have a fairly detailed description of his throne in Scripture. Made of ivory, overlaid with gold, Solomon's throne was approached by six steps, with a lion on either side of each step. The back was carved with the figure of a bull's head, the symbol of strength. Two lions stood beside the armrests. Since these lions were mentioned separately from the others, it has been suggested that these were real, live lions. Twelve carved lions, maybe even winged lions or cherubim, and possibly two live lions. Fourteen lions, six steps, ivory, gold—the ancient throne of a small kingdom sounds magnificent, but it pales in comparison to the God's throne.

His throne is "high and lifted up."

If you are "high and lifted up," people have to look up to see you. They are down and you are up, high and exalted. Perhaps that's why England's royal family (their royal *highnesses*) wave at their subjects from their *balcony*, not their front porch. When you are part of a crowd looking at someone who is up high, you feel smaller, less important. Especially if that someone is *seated* on a throne.

Picture yourself being ushered into the office of the school principal at your child's school. Or your boss's office. He is seated at his desk. There is no chair for you to sit in, and he doesn't stand. Don't you feel his authority? There is something inherently unequal about standing before someone in authority who is sitting. Now picture the boss's desk up on a platform about fifteen feet above your head. How does that make you feel when it's time for your annual review?

God's throne is above all other people, all other thrones. Everyone looks up to him, and he remains seated.

Isaiah sees the Lord seated on a throne, high and lifted up, and "*the train of his robe filled the temple.*"

Where do you think the idea for a robe with a train came from? It's really a very impractical idea. Why would anyone think about sewing extra yardage on the back of his or her robe or dress? I think it's because the original King had a robe with a very long train, and we are hard-wired from the factory to admire trains on robes, to think they are great and glorious.

Perhaps, like me, you had a train on your wedding dress. Or you have seen a bride walk the aisle, her train rustling behind her like Maria's in *The Sound of Music*, and you watched her attendants arrange it properly on the stairs at the altar. Trains look awesome flowing down aisles and even better draped down stairs. As R. C. Sproul describes it in *The Holiness of God*, God's train draped down the stairs, around the pillars, past the altar, around, down, and out till it filled the whole temple. "The world has never seen such a splendid train."

No one wears a train to church or even dining out. It makes too strong a statement for even our most dressy occasions. *Well, who died and made you queen?* No one can walk too closely behind you when you wear a train. You are physically *set apart from that which is common*— the very definition of *holy*. Isaiah tried his best to describe the One who is higher than what words can capture or imaginations can picture. He is so very *other*, which is also the best word to describe the seraphim.

"Above Him stood the seraphim."

Imagine six wings, hands, feet, eyes, roaring Niagara Falls voices, and if we would see one of them, even for a minute, our faces would look like the faces at the beginning of this chapter. No one would top off their Christmas tree with one of these beautiful, terrible aliens. But even they cover their faces before a holy God. "Holy, holy, holy is the Lord Almighty," they call out to one another. Holy is who God is. No other word in Scripture is used three times in succession to describe God. He is not just holy; he is holy, *holy*, **HOLY**.

As if to put an exclamation mark on the seraph's words, *"the foundations of the thresholds shook and the temple was filled with smoke."*

Have you ever felt an earthquake?

Jack and I traveled to San Raphael Pie de la Cuesta in outback Guatemala many years ago to minister in a small church with some friends of ours, Patty and Harry Larson. We literally drove down a dry boulder-filled creek bed to get there, and I arrived bruised from being knocked about the jeep so much.

After our meeting we retired to a small room behind the church, but I could not get to sleep. Even at two o'clock in the morning dogs were barking, and roosters were crowing. The animals seemed as uncomfortable as I was. I heard a rumble, and the bed began to vibrate. I elbowed Jack. "What's that?"

Jack sleeps hard. "It's just a big truck going by."

Yes, I could just see a tractor-trailer rig bouncing over the three-foot boulders in that creek bed. The vibrating turned to shaking. I sat bolt upright. "Harry, Patty, what do we DO?"

"Oh, nothing. It'll be all right," Harry mumbled. They were veterans of lots of earthquakes. I was not. Why was I the only one in a shaking bed that seemed concerned?

The shaking turned to rocking. Harry jumped out of bed and threw himself on top of his two-year-old sleeping in the bed next to his. Patty rolled out onto all fours on the floor. Jack was still oblivious. "What do I DO?" I cried. My secret wish to experience a little, tiny earthquake, just to see what it was like, was long satisfied.

Where do you run when the earth is quaking? It's not this thing that will blow by while you hide in the bathroom. Everything is moving. It's terrifying. There is nowhere to run. And if smoke had started pouring into the room, *I* would have keeled over.

Think of Isaiah, looking up at the brilliant throne, seeing the ultimate reality of the universe—God seated on his throne in splendor and majesty and the alien-beautiful, mighty seraphs crying, "Holy, holy, holy," and the thresholds shaking and smoke pouring into the room. . . . This is the moment-by-moment reality of God on his throne. And we live, I live, so oblivious, so wonder-challenged.

What does it mean for a creature to stand before the Creator? John Bunyan's classic, *Pilgrim's Progress,* begins with "a man . . . standing . . . with his face from his own house, a book in his hand, and a great burden upon his back. . . . [He opened the book] and as he read, he wept and trembled . . . and (broke out) with a lamentable cry, saying, 'What shall I do?'"[5] Just like me crying out in the middle of the earthquake.

And Evangelist answers, "Flee the wrath to come!"

So, with a huge burden of sin strapped to his back, he runs from the City of Destruction, his fingers in his ears crying, "Life, life, eternal life!" Isn't that what we all want? Life overflowing with love, meaning, and purpose, all wrapped up in joy with a ribbon of laughter? Christians and weekend pagans alike, we want Life, not wrath. Take all the pictures of wrath, thrones, and smoke on the mountain, stick them in a file, and delete it from our pursuit of happiness.

In my contemporary version of Bunyan's classic, *Pilgrim's Progress Today*, I wrestled with whether or not to use the imagery of the pilgrim staggering under a burden of sin. It is such a powerful image. But when I think about my own desires to pursue happiness apart from God, especially indulging in my entertainments and fantasies, I didn't tend to stagger under the burden of my sinful escapes as much as float above the pain and deadness of duty and resignation.

Perhaps, in a very unintentional way, floating was a consequence of my heritage of growing up with God as my foundation. The way my church taught it, I understood that forgiveness of sin and gaining heaven was the main purpose for my commitment to Christ. Once I crossed the line of faith and received assurance that my sin was forgiven and heaven was my eternal destiny, I could delete the pictures of wrath and the throne with a thankful smile. It was hard to imagine how much my sin mattered to Christ since I didn't have a vision of what it truly meant to enjoy a kingdom kind of life with him now. I grew up with such a strong view of grace that I tended to live casually, feeling kind of bad about my sin, flitting in before the throne with a quick confession before I moved on to my requests. I didn't feel my sin-guilt as painfully as Bunyan's pilgrim did.

And I don't think I was alone. It doesn't seem likely that people today would pick up a Bible, fear judgment, and run to escape. So in my story Christian doesn't struggle under a huge burden of sin. When he is captivated by endless amusement, vivid experiences, and all-about-me-ness, when he lives without the substance, or anchor, of God's character . . . he floats.

Perhaps the whole idea of facing God on his throne and the popular lie that we must try to be good enough to squeak into heaven has worn people out. Judgment Day has become a cliché—something to sort of wink and chuckle at, like we do when we watch the fiery preacher rattle the chandeliers in the movie *Pollyanna*.

These days aliens are the only very "other" powerful beings that it seems fashionable to fear. You can talk about a fear of aliens and probably find a sympathetic ear or two at the water cooler or the health club. "Who knows?" But if you talk about the fear of God on his throne . . . well . . . hmmm. . . . As *Bobos in Paradise* author, David Brooks, has written, for many of us "(living) in the moral temperate zone (our) morality doesn't seem compatible with the unrelenting horror of hell. Maybe instead of a Last Judgment, there will just be a Last Discussion."6

As Brooks goes on to explain, for those of us who place a high value on our freedom "there are varieties of happiness, distinct moralities and different ways to virtue. What's more, *no one ever really arrives at a complete answer* to the deepest questions or to faith. It is a voyage. . . ."7 And the journey is everything. The angst of "perpetual longing," of never arriving, never resting in ultimate truth or answers is worn as a badge. Proof that you are a deep thinker. Celebrated in our popular music and films. To arrive anywhere, to commit is to sell out your freedom. So we journey on and have this sense of floating through life. No firm beliefs. No anchor.

But one day we *will* arrive at the end of our journey. Nothing could be more certain. And no question will be more important than, "What will my Creator say to me when at last we meet? What will I say to him?"

According to the Bible, our journey of life ends at the throne of God. One day you and I will stand there. *And, God, we so want you to show us your heart. What is your intent? We are your creation. You are our origin. You are also our destiny. Do we shrink back and cringe before your throne?*

As God opens my eyes to really see him on his throne, I am overwhelmed by two realities I can so easily ignore.

First reality: I am exposed.

God is much more holy than I imagined. He is holy, holy, holy, and he looks right past my outward appearance straight into my heart. I am made in his image. I bear the image of his glory. Out of the new heart

Christ has given me, the real me acts out of love and unselfishness. He sees the kindnesses I have shown my family and friends and people I don't know. He sees how I love to sing his praises and study his Word. He knows how hard it has been to persevere through a lot of pain.

But I am such a "mixed bag of motives." My old nature dribbles sludge.

A little resentment at others who take the unbelievable liberty of not rising to meet my expectations. A few sweetly poisonous darts zinged at a hapless target of my displeasure. A glut of slimy, overblown self-pity when I'm disappointed . . .

Second reality: I am not in control.

I have tried to imagine my illusion of control from God's perspective. He created the universe, our galaxy and solar system, our earth. He holds it together by the power of his word. He wove me together in my mother's womb, created me to live and move and have my being in him. He gives me the air that I breathe and the ground upon which I stand. I have tried to imagine what it must look like when I ignore his power and rule.

Once I chased a little green lizard out of the house. On the front porch it turned to defy me. Opened its little red mouth at me. No growl or roar. Just a silent open-mouthed show of lizard-force, as if to say, "Look who you're messing with!" Some thanks for chasing him out alive instead of getting out my vacuum cleaner. And by comparison, God is infinitely greater to me than I am to my little green gatecrasher.

When I see God face to face on his throne, I will know his rule to the depths of my soul in an instant. He is in control. He is the *author* of Life, and that gives him the *author*ity over my life. Over nations. Over all the earth. He *sits* on a throne. I *stand* before him. *God is so much more powerful than I imagined.*

Think back to that fragile feeling we all felt on September 11, the emotion that gets drowned out in all the noise of our "Republic of Entertainment." In his introduction to Joel in *The Message*, Eugene Peterson writes, "There is a sense in which catastrophe doesn't introduce anything new into our lives. It simply exposes the moral or spiritual reality that already exists, but was hidden beneath an overlay of routine, self-preoccupation and business as usual."

We live in the illusion of control until we are touched one day by the awful unexpected—murderers in airplanes, children that don't come home, the other driver who runs a stop sign, or in my case a few cells with scrambled DNA. These things break the evil "enchantment of worldliness" and usher us right into the throne room.

Even as the defining moment of 9-11 has passed, the glimpses of reality behind it have faded. "It never happened!" scoffed one jet-setting Kuwaiti prince I read about in the newspaper within weeks of the towers' collapse. "We are still dining at the finest restaurants and going to the fashion shows. It never happened."

But something has happened. Many are responding to these glimpses, realizing, "We can't ignore God." We've hit the wall of 9-11 reality, and we *want* someone to be on the throne protecting us. We want someone strong enough to comfort us. We long for the security, but, *oh, that accountability.* Can't we have the one without the other?

As much as we long for God to show up suddenly in all his glory, as much as we would like to have our own private reassuring vision, we can see how problematic it is.

How would I respond to the King on the throne? That face that shines like the sun and that dazzling white robe? One part of me wants to fall down in wonder. Another part of me wants to take refuge in his power and wisdom in the midst of a world full of war and terror and physical pain and sorrow. Take comfort in his purposes that prevail over seemingly random invasions of illness and terror.

Yet another part of me feels out of control and exposed. Would I crumble and drop like Ezekiel? Maybe like Isaiah I would shut my mouth, clap my hand over my unclean lips. Would I want to RUN? HIDE? Get as far away as I can as fast as I can? Like those people in *Independence Day* when the power of the aliens is unleashed. Pile into cars . . . jam the freeways . . . jump on your bicycle . . . and go go go go?

The larger issue is, what does God want? If he wants a heart relationship, does he want us to fear him or love him? It seems impossible to do both. Look at all the people quaking and dropping.

How can we pursue love and intimacy with someone so "other" from ourselves? All those Israelites trembling at the foot of Mt. Sinai—

their glimpse of glory inspired a kind of holy terror, but it didn't compel most of them to love God with all their hearts and line up behind his leadership. Hearing God speak, seeing the mountain in smoke, feeling it shake didn't connect them to God's heart.

I always thought I loved God. And I did love him as much as I could from the middle of my tap-dancing dreams and disappointments. But even living on the forgiven side of the line of faith, I didn't really feel intimate with or passionate about him. I couldn't imagine the way God wants us to know and care about him, or the way he knows and cares about us.

How can God show himself to us in a way we can love and enjoy? How can we imagine a God so passionate about us? And why focus our imaginations on a vision of a God so powerful, so holy, so other? Doesn't that take us in the other direction?

God knows how threatening the throne can be. Perhaps that is why he shows it so sparingly— in all of Scripture just a glimpse here and a short scene there. But it is that glimpse of the throne that serves as the background against which yet another picture blazes ever more brightly.

FROM THE THRONE TO THE CROSS

*People are prepared for everything except for the fact that
beyond the darkness of their blindness there is a great light . . . the
coming together of God in his unending greatness and man
in his unending littleness, prepared for the possible,
but rarely for the impossible.*
FREDERICK BUECHNER

W hat seems an impossible dilemma is really the set-up for an
astonishing display of the glory of God's heart. If we want to see
his heart, let's back up the tape a moment to see how he responded to
the people quaking and dropping. When the disciples climbed the
mountain with Jesus and saw him transformed and heard the Father's
voice declaring his love and pleasure, they "fell face down to the
ground, terrified." In Revelation John "fell at his feet as though dead."
What was Jesus' response? It wasn't stern or angry. Nor passionless. It
was not patrician or aloof. Not the celebrity basking in and acknowledging the crowd's frenzied applause: "Thank you. Over there, thank
you."

I am captivated by the vision: In both scenes Jesus drew near. He bent over. That hand reached out and touched those shaking, quaking shoulders. A transfigured Christ "came and *touched*" his trembling friends. A risen Christ "placed his right *hand*" on John. In order to touch one who is prostrate on the ground, you have to bend over, so that when you speak, you are practically whispering in the person's ear.

The one on the throne bends over and comes near. He whispers, "Don't be afraid."

Because God is holy, he rules in justice.

Because God is love, he bends down in grace and mercy.

That is the bearing and expression of the face of the one on the throne. Grace and mercy. Although Jesus was the Son of God, although he shared the throne from eternity past, the day came when he stooped down. Made himself nothing. When all that glory on the throne was miraculously given up, the essence compressed into a tiny seed, and a servant-God grew for nine months in the darkness of Mary's womb.

God does not sit on his throne aloof and indifferent. He loves us with an ache and comes after us with delight in his eyes.

But the enemy is the great seducer. "You can't trust him," he whispers. "He's the judge and a hard one at that. If he really loves you, why all these tears? Why such a mess in your life? Your best hope for the life you want is in this world." The "evil enchantment of worldliness" clouds our thinking and desires. We seek the treasure here.

Because God is holy, our guilt and indifference separate us from his presence. It's not that he needs to say, "Go away. You don't belong here." It's the nature of things. We cannot belong when our eyes are opened to see his brilliant, pristine splendor.

Because God is love, he longs to have his family back. And he does not sit on his throne in heaven with his hands in his lap. He bends over. He descends.

God loves the world and gave his only Son.

Jesus gave up his magnificent throne to *seek and save us.*

And we desperately need to be saved. He knows how our sin keeps us from discovering and experiencing what a treasure he is. He knows it sabotages our joy and will destroy us forever. So Jesus Christ willingly offered his life to take upon himself the wrath of God so that it would not have to fall upon a heart that knows to do right, but (sigh) just wants what it wants anyway.

Surely the best way we can grasp a clearer vision of God is by seeing the Technicolor reality of God made flesh. And to focus on the picture that gives the clearest vision of his heart—Christ on the cross. Stand with me at the foot of the cross. Come close. So close that when we look up, all we can see is that face. The arms outstretched, the hands barely visible in our peripheral vision.

What do we see?

If you saw Mel Gibson's *The Passion of the Christ*, you no doubt took away indelible images of the physical pain and agony of Jesus' death on a Roman cross. In our imaginations we see the nails and the stretching, hanging, and suffocating, and we are astonished that anyone would willingly give up a throne to submit to such excruciating torture.

On the day he died, Jesus endured so much physical pain; yet the Scriptures say he didn't open his mouth. Like a lamb going to the slaughter, he endured silently the scourging, mocking, spitting, slapping, nailing, the struggle to breathe.

But at the crucial juncture, Gibson's movie could not show us, nor can we even imagine the greater pain of being cursed—being totally removed from the presence of God. Around noon something beyond all imagination began to happen.

The world went dark, and Christ became sin.

Even if we had been standing at the foot of the cross with John and Mary, we might no longer have been able to see Jesus. But we could hear him. Jesus took God's wrath upon himself, and the Father cut him off. Although he suffered all the betrayal, mocking, nails, and hanging in silence, the forsaking was more than he could bear. Finally he screamed, "My God, my God, why have you forsaken me?"

Everyone reading these pages has probably experienced the pain of being cut off from someone we love. The phone rings. Our loved one has died. My friend Vivian stood by her father-in-law's bedside and heard him draw his last breath. The spouse we cherished moves out. A son or a daughter runs away, and we don't know where our beloved child is. Death, separation. We know something of the pain. I can remember breaking up with a young man I loved very much. After our final conversation, we both drove to our separate apartments. When he reached his exit, his car veered right while mine veered left. I felt so cut off, watching his taillights disappear, my tears turning to sobs.

In his book, *Saved from What?* R. C. Sproul gives us a glimpse of Christ's pain. "There were thousands who died on crosses and may have had more painful deaths than that of Christ. But only one person has ever received the full measure of the curse of God while on a cross. I doubt Jesus was even aware of the nails and the spear—He was so overwhelmed by outer darkness. On the cross, Jesus was in the reality of hell."[8] Totally cut off from the grace and presence of God.

Second Corinthians 5:21 (NIV) tells us, "God made him who had no sin to be sin for us." What could it mean for the holy Son of God to be made sin? I've wondered if he became, if he entered into, our thoughts and feelings of anger and lust—the state of our hearts on the worst days of our lives—at the darkest moments of our sin and self-ishness. If he became the sexual rage of a Ted Bundy and the cold, maniacal bloodthirst of Hitler. If he became the guilt that washed over Judas and the horror of regret and torment of every soul in hell. If those thoughts and feelings invaded his righteous soul, and his own responses of grief and horror added to his pain. Whatever it was, it made the physical pain pale by comparison.

Sproul writes, "At the moment Christ took upon himself the sin of the world, He became the most grotesque, most obscene mass of sin in the history of the world."[9] He was completely cut off from God and every good gift in the world.

No wonder Christ screamed.

In Gibson's movie, the earthquake is a mild tremble, the darkness brief. But in reality, the earth shook so that tombs were opened, and the faithful dead walked out. The darkness and the curse, the wrenching of Jesus' soul from the life of his Father, ground on for hours. Finally, around three o'clock he cried, "It is finished." The darkness faded. Jesus' spent, bloody face became visible again. He was still breathing, strain-ing to raise himself up on his nailed feet and gasping for air. "It was over," Sproul writes. "What was over? His life? The pain of the nails?

No. It was the forsakenness that ended. The curse was finished. The light of God's countenance returned."[10] With a final push Jesus managed one last breath and said, "Into your hands I commit my spirit."

Can you see these two pictures of our Technicolor God?

God on the throne. God on the cross.

The two richest, weightiest realities in the universe.

When we stand at the foot of the cross and think of the Lamb moving down the steps of his lofty throne, leaving the cries of the seraphim behind, shedding his splendid robe, walking through the smoke and the quaking thresholds . . . When we think of him being stripped naked, lying down on the cross—bloody and throbbing—spreading his arms for the nails, and being made sin and forsaken, when we see his eyes welling up . . . *You have no idea how much I love you* . . . how do we respond?

I think of how I would feel if it were my husband or my father hanging there naked, sacrificing himself for me. The thought of so much pain and humiliation inflicted on one I love takes my breath away. That he would take it only to spare me the agony overwhelms me. The knowledge that my Creator God left his throne, was beaten to a bloody, unrecognizable pulp, and became a horrific mass of my sin takes me only so far down a road of understanding until my finite mind stalls out. I cannot comprehend it. I can only look up and see "sorrow and love flow mingled down," and let it wash over me.

He loves me so much more than my father or my husband. What does it mean to have that much love and desire envelop me?

God is so much more love than I imagined. I am loved, no matter what.

I am loved with the kind of love like when your child breaks your heart, and you throw your arms around him or touch his hand through a prison glass and know that you love him through the grief and pain, and nothing he could do could ever change your father-love or mother-love. What are the worst things you've ever done? God desires me in spite of the lies I've told, in spite of the way I've loved things and used people. In spite of the cracking of my critical whip. Jesus' sorrow and love flows over me—his child and his enemy—and makes peace between God and me. No matter what.

What else does the reality of God on the cross mean for us?

God longs to stoop down and show mercy, no matter what.

I have struggled to take the measure of God's mercy. The pictures of God I grew up with blazed with justice, and I am living proof that the way we see God colors everything in our lives. I have tended to look at life with eyes of justice more often than with mercy. We were a law-and-order family who attended a law-and-order church. Mercy hearts and do-gooders were automatically suspect.

When I read the definitions of *justice* (righteousness; conforming to what is morally good) and *mercy* (compassionate forbearance shown toward someone who is not morally good), I tend to think of them as opposites. When you think of God, how do you think of him? More justice? More mercy?

One way I have been living my way to a clearer vision of mercy is by walking through a fiery ordeal with a friend. A few years ago we sat in a Barnes and Noble cafe, and she opened her heart to me: "Late one night we received a call that our son was in county jail," she said, "charged with first-degree murder. He shot and killed his wife's ex-husband in a parking lot in broad daylight."

My friend's only child, a high school honor student and an Annapolis grad, had been serving as a special ops officer in the navy. He had been married a little over a year to a beautiful girl with a wounded heart. She had been married before, but after years of abuse she fled her husband with her two precious little girls and divorced him. Eventually, she met my friend's son at the singles class in their church.

After they were married, the girls would visit their biological father, but only with supervised visitation privileges. Their mother and her husband (my friend's son) believed that the biological father was a potential danger to the girls. My friend's son and his wife were in a custody dispute, and the biological father was seeking unsupervised visitation. It appeared they might lose.

So her son permanently removed the threat.

My eyes welled up with tears. I couldn't believe what I was hearing. It was a nightmare. Even worse, it was my dear friend's everyday reality.

It took two and a half years for the young man's case to come to trial. For two and a half years I prayed with my friend for him. Of course, in her mother's heart, she was crying out for mercy for her son. She was devastated by the crime he had committed. All she could do was offer up her son on an altar of prayer. Here I was, this law-and-order type, and as I wrestled with how to pray, my prayer became, "Lord, show her son your perfect balance of justice and mercy."

But as I prayed that prayer, I struggled even more. My heart cried out, "Lord, where *is* that perfect balance between justice for a young man who has committed murder and mercy for one who desired to protect his broken family and mercy for my friend's broken heart?"

I ached for my friend. There are many ways to lose a child, and my friend was walking through a loss loaded with humiliation. She travels and speaks a great deal, constantly meeting new people. "Oh, tell us about your family." Suddenly that casual, sweet, get-to-know-you question became salt in an open wound.

Being the mother of an only child, also a son, I couldn't imagine what it was like to have your son's wife of one year and her two daughters home for the holidays, but not your son—the main connection between your life and theirs. My friend sent pictures of her daughter-in-law and the girls that Christmas. The girls glowed with Christmas spirit. Their mother smiled, but her eyes stared out of the photos with hard pain and grief.

I couldn't imagine what it would be like to try to visit your son behind glass when you have to shout to be heard, squeezed between people on both sides also shouting at their loved ones. I couldn't imagine what it would be like for my friend's daughter-in-law to carry on alone and raise her two precious girls without a father.

In my prayers I traced the outlines of my pictures of God:

On his throne, ruling in justice—and that justice satisfied by the merciful sacrifice of God the Son on the cross. Isn't that a picture of the perfect *balance* of justice and mercy? That's certainly what I've often thought. At the same time I was praying, I was reading a book by John Piper that draws the most beautiful, compelling portrait of our Savior, *Seeing and Savoring Jesus Christ.*

And one day he spoke truth to my law-and-order heart. Piper made the case that God's justice is "essential," but his mercy is "paramount." He cited John 3:17: "God did not send the Son into the world to judge the world, but that the world might be saved through him." "If justice can be preserved," Piper wrote, "it is the apex of glory to show mercy."[11]

Romans 15:8-9 tells us that Christ came into the world "to confirm the promises given to the fathers and for the Gentiles to glorify God for his mercy." Piper explained, "*The substitutionary death of Christ created the backdrop of justice where justifying mercy would shine with unparalleled glory*" (emphasis mine).[12]

That picture I've had of God as this perfect balance of justice and mercy? It's not true. At the cross God tips the needle way over to the mercy side.

This was one of those "Aha!" moments in life when the light of "the Lord our God is merciful and forgiving" broke through the clouds of my mercy-challenged background.

We long for a just ruler to put things right and punish evil. As Peter Berger has put it, "Deeds that cry out to heaven also cry out for hell." Satan and sin need to be destroyed—sunk into a deep, dark abyss. Cast into hell, never to reign or even serve, only suffer a long, slow eternal destruction. But as we read the prophets, we see that God longs to be merciful and shower his people, shower me, with mercy. I look up at that face on the cross and see . . . our salvation is a gift of sheer pity. He does not long to "make us pay" for all the stupid, selfish things we do. No matter what.

I called my friend and confessed my misled prayers and thoughts. My mercy-corrected pictures of God on the throne and God on the cross blazed. This struggle to pray for my friend has been a watershed in my life. Instead of looking so hard for justice, I find myself looking for ways to show mercy, mercy, mercy. We still pray for God's mercy to find my friend's son, who is serving a life sentence in prison without parole. And we see God at work. (You can read my friend's story in *When I Lay My Isaac Down*, by Carol Kent.)

Whatever we may think or feel about God on the throne should only bring us to God on the cross where we find:

God's love shines even brighter than his justice.
Mercy beyond imagining.
Our God is a lover and a giver. He gave himself.
He stoops down and touches us and asks,
"Will you love me back? I have so much more to give you!"

Three days after Jesus died on the cross, God threw death in reverse and resurrected him. In "The Weight of Glory," Lewis writes, "We are in need of the strongest spell possible to break the evil enchantment of worldliness." There is no stronger spell than the power of resurrection. The power to change anger and tears and end-of-the-world grief into dancing, hugging laughter in a split second. For the joy set before him, for the prospect of Easter wonder, Jesus endured the cross, scorning its shame, and now he is seated at the right hand of the throne of Majesty where he will judge the nations.

We will never actually stand before the cross, but we will stand before the throne. We've been asking the question, "How would we respond?" Even more important is the question, "How does God want us to respond?"

Hebrews 4:16 (NIV) gives us the answer. We are offered an amazing invitation: "Let us then approach the throne of grace with confidence, so that we may receive mercy and find grace to help us in our time of need."

We are invited to come to the throne "with confidence." The King James renders it "boldly." The opposite of terror and trembling. We approach with our heads up and a relaxed, confident stride. We gaze fully into his face with eyes that mirror the delight in his, the way a bride walks down the aisle to her bridegroom.

Perhaps like me, there are times in your life when you are so unwilling to submit to God. "But, God, I can't trust you. I have to hold on to this man, this job, this friend, this child, this deal, this position, this grudge, this dream, this escape to survive, to feel loved and valued. I can't give this to you. I can't give you my life. It's the only thing I've got. I'll lose everything."

What we have here is a failure to imagine! The King invites us to embrace the cross and kneel at his throne with something so much greater in mind: He doesn't want to rob us of anything. He is the giver.

He wants to shower us with mercy, give us his grace to help in every need. And there is so much more.

In Revelation 3:21 (NIV) God promises us, "To him who overcomes, I will give the right to sit with me on my throne, just as I overcame and sat down with my Father on his throne."

Words cannot capture how astonishing this reality will be. Far from wanting to dominate or diminish us, God promises that we will share his throne, his reign with him. What a great irony! We pull back from God because we want to sit on the throne of our own life, write the lead in our own small story. And he wants us to kneel at his throne so he can invite us to rise and join him in his reign of the universe.

Can you truly understand how amazing that is? It's as if one day I'm shopping at Dillard's, and Ralph Lauren himself asks me if I want to share his design empire and his label, "Lauren and Lael."

Or one day the President calls and asks me if I would please consider governing the blue states because he just wants to manage the red ones.

We laugh. How preposterous. Unthinkable. Silly.

And yet we read the unfailingly true, always-comes-to-pass Word of God telling us, "This is my vision for you—to sit on my throne and reign with me." And we think, *Reigning. Well, okay . . .*

No, it is utterly *amazing!* We should be laughing in wonder. Exchanging *Can you even believe this?* glances. Why would he do such a thing?

Because that's the kind of God he is.

And that is the point, much more than the reigning.

Can you even imagine, just a little? The King wants you and me to share his throne. He wants to exalt us, just like he exalted his Son. In our worst moments of lust and anger Jesus died for us. And now he stoops down. He touches us. The King comes near. "Come reign with me for eternity!" he whispers. Our hesitancy and fear melt. He grabs our hand and invites us into his laughter.

If we go back to those scenes of people quaking and dropping before God in his glory, God on the throne, we discover something else about how God wants us to see him and respond to him. Not only is Jesus bending down, touching, whispering, "Don't be afraid." He issues an invitation: "Get up!"

Isaiah is cringing, crying, "I've got such a mouth!" But God's response is the ultimate "one-minute reprimand": "This coal has cleansed your mouth. Now it's taken care of. Don't wallow. Don't get taken out by false guilt. People need your ministry. Let's move forward."

Ezekiel is over in Babylon, down by the river, probably feeling as far from God as you can get. Listening to the people wail brutal songs about the Babylonian soldiers who dashed their babies' heads against the rocks. And God's throne blows in—a fiery glow in the midst of an immense windstorm. God's mobile throne. Mounted above four living creatures—all wings and faces and wheels within wheels covered with eyes, darting back and forth like flashes of lightning. And (of course!) Ezekiel is laid out. But God wants to talk with him. "Get up!" God's Spirit lifts him back to his feet. "Son of Man, I have an assignment for you. People need your ministry. Let's go."

If we are in Christ Jesus, there is no condemnation at the throne (Rom. 8:1). One of Satan's great coups is to create an automatic link in our imaginations between "God's throne" and "God's condemnation" and leave us in bondage to our painful awareness of our sin.

The writer of Hebrews insists that we see a different picture on the screens of our imagination. You have *not* come to a mountain burning with fire—to darkness, gloom, and the voice that terrified the people of Israel. That is not the picture you are to imagine.

Instead, you have come to "the heavenly Jerusalem, the city of the living God" with "thousands upon thousands of angels in joyful assembly, to the church of the firstborn, whose names are written in heaven. You have come to God, the judge of all men, to the spirits of righteous men made perfect, to Jesus the mediator of a new covenant, and to the sprinkled blood" (12:22-24 NIV).

If Isaiah 6 is the close up, Hebrews 12 gives us the wide-angle picture of what it means to come to God on his throne. Last night I watched the NBA final championship game and couldn't help but think that the scene as we boldly approach God's throne *is so much more joyful than I imagine*. The stands will be filled with celebrating angels. If the two seraphs sounded like Niagara Falls, what will thousands upon thousands sound like? The players are the church, honored by name.

We'll find ourselves in the company of Moses and Luther and George Washington and C. S. Lewis and other people who share our loves and dreams and Lord.

We tend to think of our salvation as our justification, the fact that Jesus' sprinkled blood will cover our sins. Yes, the sprinkled offering will be there, but we are to imagine life with Jesus and his saints and a kingdom that can't be shaken.

So we worship, we *worship* with reverence and awe. Not God as my foundation for my nice Christian life. We worship with awe and come boldly before that throne and find mercy and grace.

The throne of God is Command and Control of the Universe, the hub of worship and judgment in Revelation. But the throne is also a place of intimacy and relationship. The mercy that flows down from the cross, flows from the throne as well. God invites us to join him there for a new challenge, a new adventure. And he is saving a spot beside him on that high, exalted, gleaming sapphire rainbow-radiance throne in anticipation of that day . . .

If you have never seen this picture of Christ, risen and radiant, then come to him for a long look. Fix your undistracted gaze on him— on the cross, on the throne. Wait there. He offers you an invitation to the Life you long for—a life of joy, blessing, and forgiveness. Accept his finished work of salvation.

It is not enough to merely look at the picture or mentally check off the truth of this reality. By faith in Jesus Christ we receive his sacrifice for us on the cross and enter into a real relationship with him and a new "kingdom kind of life." And just as our sin became his reality, his righteousness becomes our reality.

In Bunyan's original story of *The Pilgrim's Progress*, the man approaches the foot of the cross, carrying his great burden on his back, desperate to be rid of it. And there is this wonderful, magical symbolism: At his sight of the cross the burden falls off and tumbles down the hill into an open sepulcher, and he sees it no more.

What a marvelous picture of what happens the moment we put our faith in Jesus Christ—the burden of our true moral guilt before a holy

God falls away into the empty tomb. And this is the invitation—to receive his gift of forgiveness and follow him into a new life of blessing today.

No matter how great your burden, it will tumble into the open sepulcher.

No matter how long you've been floating, you can find solid ground.

Maybe you have already embraced Christ. But today the King who loves you is whispering, "You are living so casually. Have you been distracted, living life in the shallows, forgetting my desire for you, caught up in your small story? Floating again? Where is your delight and passion in seeking me? Am I only the foundation in your life?"

Sometimes I wonder . . .

How would our lives be different if we began everyday in Hebrews 12, boldly approaching the throne? Eager to worship with our time, our talents? Ready for our assignments? Delighting in that voice and touch?

Good morning, Father. I begin my day in the City of the Living God, with thousands upon thousands of angels in joyful assembly and the company of those men and women I so admire. I want you to burn this picture of your power and splendor and love on my heart today. Thank you that I can approach you with boldness and go out with courage. Thank you for the power you give me to love well and show others this treasure of grace you have poured into my heart. Lord, I am in such desperate need of your mercy to do it. When life in a fallen world doesn't even register a two on my soaring scale of expectations, help me imagine all you are and all you plan to give me. Help me live present to your face on the throne moment by moment.

How would our lives be different if we ended each day before the throne—covered by that love and mercy that takes away our sin and defeats the enemy's power over us?

Ah, Lord, I'm like Isaiah—I have such a mouth. I'm like Ezekiel, feeling beat up and so far from you. Let your love and mercy cover me. Take the pieces of my broken dreams and bind them up. Take this heart of stone, so determined to shield and protect, and make it a tender heart of flesh.

*Help me to see that I can be broken as you were and soar to new life and
laughter as you did.*

When I survey the throne and the wondrous cross, when my imagination burns with the terrible beauty of my God, I think, *How can I
not love and enjoy a God like that?* It should be enough, shouldn't it?
"Love so amazing" ought to keep us loving and worshiping and never
wavering.

7

ACCIDENTAL
TOURISTS

I don't know if we each have a destiny,
or if we're all floatin' around accidental-like on the breeze.
But I, I think maybe it's both.
FORREST GUMP

But then there's the infamously depressing second law of spiritual
dynamics in a fallen universe: All my passion and energy toward
God tends toward entropy—disorganization, lack of focus, weeds,
rust. Today's vision is tomorrow's deadline panic. Today's passion is
tomorrow's numbed-out commute or chauffeur service from school to
ballet to soccer practice to homework and bedtime. Even when we
carry the pictures of the throne and the cross in our hearts, we have to
recapture our astonishment, live our way to a deeper grasp of what they
mean today. How does that happen?

"You will seek me and find me when you seek me with all your
heart" (Jer. 29:13 NIV). *God grows our vision for him when we seek him*
with all our hearts.

But we tend to seek other things just a bit more.

Ask a group of friends or a classroom of students: What are you passionate about? What or who delights you beyond all else? "God," or "God's kingdom," or "heaven" rarely top the list.

How did you decide what to do after high school? Where to go to college? Where to work? Whom to marry? What church to attend? What life mission to pour yourself into? Surely, if I had been seeking God with all my heart, my life's journey would have been more to the point much earlier.

Instead I was an "accidental tourist," taking in a performance here and a relationship there, pursuing the pleasure of my heart within "acceptable Christian boundaries." For the most part. My decision of where to attend college is a good case in point: During my senior year in high school a friend attending Southern Methodist University invited me to enjoy a Young Life reunion weekend together. Smitten by the weekend of fun, fellowship, and freedom, I immediately applied and was accepted.

A month later one of my high school friends asked me to room with her at Texas Christian University, where her sister fixed us up with dashing college men. My SMU friend was now engaged, and TCU with a roommate in hand looked more appealing—a plan that lasted for several months until another friend who attended the University of Texas at Austin invited me to visit her.

This is where it gets very Blonde. I loved the BIGNESS of 40,000 students crammed into that famous forty acres. I had a dazzling good time with my friend's friends. My best friend from church asked me to room with her. In the small print of my college search specs it counted for something that all three schools were top tier universities, and UT's Spanish department, my intended major, was nationally ranked.

To Austin I went.

Throughout the decision process I prayed for wisdom. But really the people connections and that old "enchantment of worldliness" were the determining factors. In my churched Blonde heart, "Where will we have the most fun with friends . . . of course, with *Christian* friends?" was true north on my compass of life decisions.

My informal polling finds it's the same for many. When we are free to choose beyond the bounds of necessity, we aim for a certain lifestyle, a certain marriage pool. We go to college to find or be with friends. Or recreate. One friend loved the mountains but hated the cold. He pulled out a map to find the southern-most campus with mountains and headed to Flagstaff. Another fellow I heard of selected Appalachia State because it was the number two "bouldering" campus in the nation. We select a course of study that complements our social lives. I have a brilliant friend who went to Harvard but chose an English major because he didn't want to work too hard.

One of my friends dreamed of finding a husband and career. Kids were secondary. Another dreamed of having kids. The husband was secondary. We find a team we want to work with. Perhaps we are more goal-oriented. We choose our college and career with a great ten- or twenty-year plan in view. Perhaps, like I did, we even sign on for kingdom ministry. But do we really seek God and his kingdom first? With all our hearts? With a passion that shapes every decision?

If someone could just write *The Five Easy Steps to Vision and Passion for God*, we could craft a mission statement, create a strategy, and tick off a list of action steps. Instead God tells us in Zechariah 4:6 (NIV), "'Not by might nor by power, but by my Spirit,' says the LORD Almighty."

The people living in Judah in Zechariah's time had lost their vision of God. The Babylonian hordes had sacked and pillaged Jerusalem, torched their temple, hauled off the brightest and best, and left a remnant whose identity as God's people lay shattered in the ruins. For seventy years they had been the butt of jokes around all the Mideast campfires. After seventy years of scratching out an existence, seventy years of losing seasons, God wanted to restore them as a nation. He gave his prophet Zechariah visions to fire the imaginations of his people, stir their passion, and move them into action. Zerubbabel was tapped as governor and point man on the project.

God gave Zechariah a vision specifically for Zerubbabel:

> *"I see a solid gold lampstand with a bowl at the top and seven lights on it, with seven channels to the lights. Also there are two olive trees by it, one on the right of the bowl and the other on its left." I asked the angel who talked with me, "What are these, my lord?" He answered, "Do you not know what these are?" "No, my lord," I replied. So he said to me, "This is the word of the LORD to Zerubbabel: 'Not by might nor by power, but by my Spirit,' says the LORD Almighty." (4:2-6 NIV)*

All we need to imagine God, to imagine what we can become, what we can accomplish—every impulse for that imagining is available "by my Spirit." That is Godsight.

How was God going to ignite the heart of his leader to rebuild a people that had been living small for so long? With the oil of his Spirit. Vision, imagination is energized by God's Spirit. The oil of the Spirit burned in the lamps so that the leaders could *see* God and the lamp-stand in his heavenly temple and find the passion to rebuild his earthly temple. Why rebuild the temple first? So his people could worship in his temple where the energy of the Spirit would open their eyes to see God, which would fire their passion and give them the energy to rebuild their city.

We cannot summon up this kind of vision. "Not by might nor by power." We can't do something unless we can imagine it first. But everything we need to energize our hearts to see and delight in God and imagine the mission he has for us is available "'by my Spirit,' says the LORD Almighty."

When Paul prayed for the Christians at Ephesus, he prayed that the Father would give them "the Spirit of wisdom and revelation." In the same breath he prayed "that the *eyes of your heart may be enlightened* in order that you may know the hope to which he has called you, the riches of his glorious inheritance in the saints" (1:17-18 NIV). My physical eyes send pictures to my brain. On a good day, when I'm not talking on my cell phone, my mind processes the information. But it is the eyes of my heart opened by God's Spirit that recognize the real *value* of what I can physically see. And as I receive the work of God's Spirit in my life, he opens the eyes of my heart to see . . . the *unseen*—the glorious riches of my inheritance—and value it *more* than my next new tap dance or my dream trip to England.

And I'm back to my "All right then, show me, please; just show me!" prayer, the same prayer the psalmist prayed:

"*Show us your strength, O God. . . .*" (Ps. 68:28 NIV)

"*Show us your unfailing love, O LORD. . . .*" (Ps. 85:7 NIV)

"*Open my eyes that I may see. . . .*" (Ps. 119:18 NIV)

Through his Spirit, in answer to our prayers, God opens the eyes of our hearts to Life. He illumines our options, enabling us to see the reality of choices. He is the ultimate multi-tasker, working simultaneously on many different levels—in our successes and failures, our relationships, our fun and entertainment, our loneliness in a crowd, our quiet moments with him. He is particularly busy at holidays, in crises, in risks, exposing our Blondeness and obsessions. No wonder he groans for us in prayer: "Father, this one . . . oh, this one . . . give her more grace." Jesus said the Spirit works like the wind: "you hear its sound, but you do not know where it comes from or where it goes."

Because God has created each of us with our own unique heart prints, the way God's Spirit works must be radically different from person to person. And yet we find common echoes of his blowing work. Because we are taken out by the same deceptions, we are often illuminated by the same truth. As I "empty out the pockets of my life," I catch glimpses of how the Spirit's oil has illuminated the smallness of my accidental tourism and my Blonde tap-dancing dreams. He has ignited my vision and passion for God in ways common to the ages and consistent with his Word.

More than any other means, *suffering* pops the bubble of the "evil enchantment of worldliness." It yanks back the curtain on all our distractions and helps us see the Glory. Our collective experience of the collapse of the World Trade Center confirmed this more deeply than words can ever express.

But that reality is already fading. What we have in its aftermath is a war on terror that has settled upon us like a low-grade fever. As our emotional distance from ground zero increases, the blinking neon of all our distractions resumes its former frenzy. For most of us 9-11 is no longer a suffering of great loneliness or loss.

And yet the suffering goes on for many. As I write this, it is the time of the February sweeps. One of the new shows ABC has used to troll for ratings is *Extreme Makeover: Home Edition*, the new millennium version of *Queen for a Day*. A deserving family is chosen, not just for a new washing machine, but for a complete makeover of their home. One family chosen is that of an army reservist, a loan officer called to serve in Iraq and separated from his family for almost a year. The wife is tearfully grateful, and the three young boys can hardly contain themselves. They bounce off to Disneyland for seven days while the hard hats gut their house, chop down their hedges, and make everything new.

When the family returns, the boys gape and giggle at their new castle bedroom and carwash shower. They jump up and down at their new bedroom stereos and plasma TV. But then the moment the audience knows is coming and can't wait to see finally arrives: Their dad returns from Iraq. Dressed in camo, his rucksack slung over his shoulder, he walks into the backyard.

The whooping ceases in mid-whoop. The smiles give way to gasps. The boys shoot straight into their father's arms, clinging to him in silence, eyes glowing, shimmering. All the computerized floor plans, thousands of man hours and truckloads of goodies—none of it compares to the embrace of their father's arms. Not one child says, "Wow, Dad, look at our new whiffleball court." This is not happiness of a greater degree, but joy of an infinitely different kind. Even the home improvers sense it. The hard hats brush their cheeks. The designers instinctively duck the camera. Not the least telltale sign of disappointment or offense darkens their faces. In that moment they know all their work is icing on a cake beyond their ability to prepare—an offering of joy at the real banquet. The easy camaraderie of a family circle can obscure the real glory and value of those we love. Their Dad's absence has opened the eyes of their hearts to see it.

With our super-sized signature grocery stores and a Starbucks on every corner, we take so much for granted. We do not see things as they really are. *Suffering opens the eyes of our hearts to see more of God than we ever imagined.* Upon the screens of our imagination play not just the dreams of what we hope for, but also our illusions of life—about God, about where life is found, about ourselves. The Spirit is at work "disillusioning" us, as Oswald Chambers describes it, illuminating the reality beyond the dark glass.

I was living so small in my early adult years. But the changes in my life and dreams came not so much from seeking God with all my heart, but from the fact that he grabbed hold of me in a black hole of pain.

Sometimes suffering brings a great clarity of vision. But the loss of my health in Costa Rica bewildered me. *Lord, I'm going to the mission field with my husband. I'm laying down my dreams to follow you and trust-ing you to use me, fill my heart. I choose you over my own tap-dancing dreams and you allow . . . this?*

I wonder if, when I chose Jack and the mission field, God smiled. *Yes! She chose the kingdom! And I will give her . . . myself.*

In Philippians 3:8-10 Paul declared that he "suffered the loss of all things and count them as rubbish, in order that . . . I may know [Christ] and the power of his resurrection, and may share his suffer-ings, becoming like him in his death. . . ." The sufferings of choosing God and winding up in pain help us to become like Christ. Isn't that what we long for? *Lord, I want to know you and be like you!*

But with the onset of rheumatoid arthritis I did not feel more Christlike. I didn't see that I was becoming more like him. When I caught a glimpse of myself in the mirror, I saw a stooped and weary creature, puffed by prednisone, elbows contracted, fingers knotted and swollen. I could see my world shrink as surely as Alice's down the rabbit hole—a life of chronic disease and pain. No cure. I turned my questions over and over in my head. Back in the States, as I shuf-fled across campus to complete my graduate studies, I felt the weight of a worldview that denies God squeezing my faith. I would crawl into bed each night and cling to a God who often felt distant. But like Peter, where else was there to go? *Jesus, only you have the words of eternal life.*

As I peruse my picture albums from our early years of marriage, I see a couple absorbing the pain and limitations and moving on. A fam-ily finding a new normal in the routine of full-time ministry, caregiv-ing, and preschool, spiced up by gatherings at Grandmother's and Mad Hatter birthday parties.

When I ask myself, "How did God grow my vision for him and his kingdom through the early years of rheumatoid arthritis?" I can say that God showed me he was not the God I thought he was. Living with a big NO to your prayers changes your simple view of God. I realized that if you deposit a choice for obedience, you don't automatically withdraw a check for answered prayer. I realized you can pray with all the faith you can muster and still have to live with a big NO. I realized what sovereignty means in life, not just on paper.

Pain dis-illusions us. Our idea of God takes a beating. In *A Grief Observed*, C. S. Lewis writes, "My idea of God is not a divine idea. It has to be shattered time after time. He shatters it himself. He is the great iconoclast. Could we not almost say that this shattering is one of the marks of his presence?"[13]

Iconoclasm, shattering images, is painful. I think the distance from God I felt in those early years was at least in part due to that shattering Presence. It was hard to feel intimate with someone always lugging a sledgehammer. Like Job, my "wonder was too small," and I discovered *God is much greater than I ever imagined*.

I have watched friends take a big NO to their prayers and desperately hold on to a cracked image of God. They believe that God answers YES if only you have enough faith; so obviously the problem is their lack of it. Paul's thorn is a pesky footnote on their theology. They labor to confess everything they can think of; they put anyone who suggests they may not get a YES at arms' length, and finally it is their spirits that crack and shatter under the weight of the faulty icon of God they carry. God's yoke is easy, and his burden is light, and he would much prefer we let the image go.

The more I saw of God's greatness and sovereignty and inscrutability, the more I settled into duty and resignation. But his Spirit can leverage anything to expand our vision. As my heart escaped my pain and limitations into evenings of entertainment and occasional fantasy, my soul and vision shrank to the point where I was desperate for more. More room, more purpose, more impact . . . MORE! The very celebrities whose work and lives I enjoyed showed mine to be so small by comparison. Whom was I impacting with my life and work? When Zach started first grade, I felt the tension even more keenly and cried out to God to give me more Life. More purpose.

Perhaps in some future private discussion God will show me how the limitations imposed by the loss of my health was a protection and a discipline. Perhaps it was the Spirit's way of passing a plateful of dangerous opportunities for a life of perpetual Blondeness and ever more ambitious tap dancing out of my grasping reach. We do not often reckon out loud the possibility that our suffering may be the result of God's discipline. In decades of small group Bible study I have never heard anyone say anything remotely like, "Yes, I think God is grounding me and taking away my car keys right now so I'll deal with my pride and pushiness." Yet Hebrews 12 assures us that if we are truly God's children, some of our suffering will be his discipline and a mark of our legitimacy. "If I didn't love you, I wouldn't take away your keys."

Jack's faithful love for me during these years was a lifesaver and his patience amazing. He would occasionally ask me if I was watching too much TV. He would meet my complaints about limited funds with tender encouragement to be grateful for God's provision. He prayed for me. And when I took a step to begin teaching a college course in Western Civilization, he supported me.

I knew my drift toward TV and fantasy was partially a default response to the reality that so many other options were beyond my physical reach. Work, recreation, regular hospitality, practical care for others like cooking meals and helping with child care—the rhythm of my friends' lives was a tune I couldn't dance to.

I could sit. So I decided to sit and read. Sit and write lessons. Sit on my desk and lecture. And I could think. I am eternally grateful that there are no joints in my head. My synapses fire without the least pain or tightness. I can create and analyze for hours and not have to lie down until the throbbing in my brain dissipates. The thing God gifted me to do, the thing he prepared me to do professionally, doesn't require a great deal of mobility or strong hands. It was all mercy, mercy, mercy that I didn't have to live out my days as a frustrated basketball coach or hair stylist.

When we're doing something we're gifted to do, it gives us energy to do the other things. The rising tide of joy in teaching again floated the boats of laundry, cooking, and cleaning. It was not enough to fill my divided heart with all that I really needed, but it soaked up an appreciable amount of TV time and daydream energy. And it was a move toward kingdom mission and preparation for the road ahead.

During these years I knew God was pressing me to give up my fantasies. When I tripped over my grandmother's antique iron and landed in the hospital with a cracked pelvis, I began to wonder about a link between my escapes and God's discipline. Two weeks in the hospital, months of recovery at home—I may have been connecting unrelated dots, but I decided to take my small disaster as a serious hint: *Let it go, Lael*. And I did.

I couldn't yet see what God wanted to give me of himself and his kingdom, but I knew what he wanted me to give up. My fantasy had become a real foothold for the enemy to have his way with me. Jesus was inviting me to put my heart where the Spirit could get at me.

> "*Whoever has my commands and obeys them, he is the one who loves me. He who loves me will be loved by my Father, and I too will love him and show myself to him.*" *Then Judas (not Judas Iscariot) said, "But, Lord, why do you intend to show yourself to us and not to the world?" Jesus replied, "If anyone loves me, he will obey my teaching. My Father will love him, and we will come to him and make our home with him.*" (John 14:21-23 NIV)

Why can't we see God on demand? Like Judas, we don't understand why Jesus doesn't show himself to the whole world. We are Americans. We require equal access, equal opportunity. *Jesus, we want to see you and your glory, NOW. We want you to show yourself to the whole world. Why do you make it conditional?* It's hard to see Jesus turn Judas' question aside. We marvel at how thousands of people lined up for *The Passion of the Christ* and saw Jesus so differently.

"No doubt God wants us to see him. . . . Love always wants to be known," writes Dallas Willard in *The Divine Conspiracy*. "But seeing is all the more difficult in spiritual things, where the objects . . . *must be willing to be seen*. Persons rarely become present where they are not heartily wanted. Certainly that is true for you and me. We prefer to be wanted, warmly wanted, before we reveal our souls—or even come to a party."[14]

Jesus and his Father show up, move in, and make a home in a heart that wants him and demonstrates the stuff of real love—prizing and choosing what he wants.

When the children of Israel were about to enter the Promised Land, Moses assembled them and said, "*Your eyes have seen all that the* LORD *did in Egypt to Pharaoh, to all his officials and to all his land. With your own eyes you saw those great trials, those miraculous signs* and great wonders. But to this day the LORD has not given you a mind that understands or *eyes that see* or ears that hear" (Deut. 29:2).

That's shocking. So much for miracles. Here are these people who did actually see God part a sea and move a mountain and still not have eyes to see and prize his glory. We don't like to think that God would ever hold out on us. If we search for clues in the story as to why the Lord was not opening the eyes of their hearts, we find Moses telling them: "For I know how rebellious and stiff-necked you are. If you have been rebellious against the LORD while I am still alive and with you, how much more will you rebel after I die!" (Deut. 31:27 NIV).

God did not give eyes to see him to a people who did not really want him.

Do we want to catch a clearer vision of Jesus? Is it possible that our fondness for our favorite distractions may be keeping us from seeing him? That our good life dreams blind us to his true worth? Do we ask God to show us where we are choosing our dreams over his and to help us to want him?

We want a vision for God that ignites our passion. But how do we take hard steps of obedience when we don't want to? Who makes the first move?

Looking back to the throne and the cross, we can see that God always makes the first move. He bends down and comes near. He approaches our small life table and offers his hand. We resist all the NO welling up inside and turn our imaginations to what he promises—that last dance in *Beauty and the Beast* where Belle and the Prince swirl around the grand hall with "happily ever after" written all over their faces. We take his hand, and he shows himself a little. We dance. He shows. We follow. One, two, three; one, two, three, and . . . eventually . . . it may take a while . . . we see his heart, and the sparks fly.

Our choices to follow Jesus don't always lead to sunlit fields of laughter and dancing. They can be a way into suffering or a way out of it.

Sometimes taking that hand leads to a sudden plot twist of suffering—like my Costa Rican sojourn. The dance can be a Romans 5 pathway into pain. Anyone who has stood at the ballet bar like I did in college trying to get my right toe pointing at three o'clock and my left toe pointing at nine o'clock with my heels together and my knees straight knows what pain is. But it's the pain that produces *Swan Lake* and *The Nutcracker*. The pain of our dance with Christ produces endurance, character, and hope "because God's love has been poured into our hearts through the Holy Spirit" (Rom. 5:5).

Pain opens a spigot or even a fire hydrant of God's love. When you ask most people, "When did you see the love of God most clearly in your life?" usually they will tell you about a time of suffering. "The LORD is close to the brokenhearted" (Ps. 34:18 NIV), even when we can't imagine it, and our hearts are too small to fully absorb it.

The process of building endurance and character and hope can be a time, like the early years of my illness, when there is such a smallness to be enlarged that most of what we feel is the stretching and snapping and hollowing out. It's standing at the bar with your toes east and west until it seems as if your hip sockets will pop out and your extended arm will fall off.

I felt a measure of God's love in my pain, certainly the rock and comfort of truth, but the tenderness of intimacy was slow in coming. It has taken years for the jet wash of God's love to dissolve the crust of worldly Blonde ambition and release the new heart he has given me to love him with anything like the fierceness of his love for me, especially when I have been slow to seek him and let him. Most of the incremental work of showing me his heart and kingdom barely registered on the screen of my imagination in those young adult years. But I look back and wonder at how well he has done it. I was the accidental tourist, but he was the captain at the helm, the cabbie who offered me a lift, and the conductor who stopped the train to let me off at the stop of his choosing.

Sometimes obedience is a way into suffering. Sometimes it opens the way into a life much larger than we could imagine.

In an amazing "coincidence," within months of turning off the TV and the fantasies, I imagined the possibilities of doing a Bible study on understanding a Christian worldview, that larger picture of life, and I began to write it. My church gave me an opportunity to teach it. In my new season of obedience and recovery from my fractured hip, I found the time I'd been wanting to write my ideas into a manuscript. Through unique circumstances and timing God brought women into my life who helped it become a book: *Worldproofing Your Kids: Helping Moms Prepare Their Kids to Navigate Today's Turbulent Times.* Was there a direct connect between a decision of obedience and the privilege of teaching and writing? The main reason I think so is because, through the process of writing, God showed me so much more of his heart and his kingdom.

In the months of study and writing, God showed me not just himself, but pictures of the kingdoms of this world, not their splendor but their brokenness. I deeply processed our society's loss of confidence in Truth for all people for all time, our loss of faith that we are created in God's image and the trickle-down effects on the care and respect we give the weakest among us. I took the measure of our "Republic of Entertainment" and its conditioning effect on everything from our five-second attention spans to our vision for life. And I realized as never before that *the glory of this world is so much emptier than I imagined.*

The more I wrote about a larger vision for life, the more my own vision grew. I smile at God's timing. Was there a connection between laying down my fantasies and opening my eyes to see "my glorious inheritance"—my future with him? As I was researching heaven for the last chapter of the book, I looked through the scriptural gates, and the reality dazzled me. I could see the City, and that is when I discovered the place God had saved for me beside him on his throne. The transforming power of a clearer vision of heaven is so great that it deserves an entire chapter later on.

God is constantly wooing and inviting us, even when we are holding out on him. When I was still flirting with my fantasy, he opened the door to teaching, the pathway to my present kingdom ministry. I used to think as a single that I needed to make at least a 90 in Spirituality 101 before God would bring a godly husband along. I didn't score that high. Just as "Jesus looked at (the rich young ruler) and *loved* him," he saw beyond my tap-dancing Blondeness to the person he would grow me to be. He lavishes grace while still inviting us, "You have no idea how much more Life I want to offer you!"

How do you count your blessings? I was actually asked to list my blessings once for a professional leadership evaluation, shake down my grudging memory and hand over the high points, the most meaningful moments in each stage of my life. The list looked much like the Old Testament blessings delivered to the people of Israel gathered on Mount Gerizim: blessings on our family, blessings on my work and ministry, blessings on our house, the comings and goings of our calendar, and the storehouses of our bank account and IRAs.

But I've come to wonder what Jesus would make of my list. Maybe most of those were just the dinner rolls and celery sticks, and the real banquet of blessings, the Steak Diane and the Bananas Foster, were the moments of pain and emptiness that drove me to seek and choose him. I think about Jesus' blessings, his "beatitudes," given from another mountain in Israel: blessings in my frustration and despair, my mourning, my longing for everything to be put right. I am blessed in these longings and pains because *I will see God* and taste his kingdom, and that is by far the greatest blessing he has to give.

When I have asked others, "How did God open the eyes of your heart and torch your desire for him and his kingdom? How did he enlarge your passion for truth as precepts and principles to become a passion for the reality of his presence?" I hear their stories of suffering and choosing God even when everything within them wants their own way. I also hear about people of vision who share with us what the eyes of their hearts have seen—the kingdom kind of Life shining on the screens of their imaginations.

8

TWENTY-TWENTY
IMAGINATION

Being saved and seeing Jesus are not the same thing.
Many are partakers of God's grace who have never seen Jesus.
When once you have seen Jesus, you can never be the same,
other things do not appeal as they used to.
OSWALD CHAMBERS, *MY UTMOST FOR HIS HIGHEST*

Guinevere (Julia Ormond) paces the bare castle room; the broken pieces of her honor crackle under her feet. Approaching footsteps echo down the stone corridor. The bolt is thrown back. King Arthur (Sean Connery) strides into the room, dismissing his escort. The air between them is crowded with betrayal, shame, desire. He gathers himself, struggling against everything rising in his heart. Her eyes steady, her body taut, she faces him, her chest barely moving as she breathes. Arthur forces his feelings into the words of a man who is also a king:

"I ask you not to lie to me even if you think you'll hurt me. . . . Have you given yourself to him?"

"No, my lord."

"Do you love him?"

"Yes."

"How did I fail you?"

"You've not failed me, my lord."

"I saw your face as you kissed him."

"Love has many faces. I may look on you differently, but not with less love."

"When a woman loves two men, she must choose between them."

"I choose you."

"Your will chooses me! Your heart chooses him."

"Then you have the best of it. My will is stronger than my heart. Do you think I put so high a price on my feelings? Feelings live for a moment and the moment passes. My will holds me steady to my course through life."

What do you think? Has she given him "the best of it"?

After a hard day of obedience, I can picture myself having this conversation (from the movie *First Knight*) with God. "Lael, have you given yourself to another lover?"

"Given myself?" It takes me back to the first time I read Francis Schaeffer's *True Spirituality* and my revulsion at the picture Schaeffer made so clear: "It is possible, even after we are Christians, to put ourselves into the arms of someone else and bring forth his fruit in this world." My little escapes that seem so innocent can be more than dining with the devil, more like falling into his arms and letting him have his way with me.

"No, my Lord."

What a relief. It was a battle. I flirted with my escape. I longed for the relief, but I didn't cross the line.

My will held me steady.

It is a mark of highest Christian maturity to trust and obey God regardless *of our feelings.* To follow him because he is God, Lord of all the universe, and we are his creation. The way Noah built the ark when he had to be stuffing his questions, like "What is rain? What is a flood?" The way Mary yielded to God's plan when she loved Joseph and a sudden pregnancy was bound to rewrite the script for their wedding. I love the way Eugene Peterson put it in his classic, *A Long Obedience in the Same Direction*: "We can act ourselves into a new way of feeling much quicker than we can feel ourselves into a new way of acting."

However, many in the church have inherited from the reason-is-everything Enlightenment a slightly amended view: *It is a mark of highest Christian maturity to trust and obey God* and disregard *our feelings.* To count them as a tiny four-point footnote on the main thing: obedience. The difference is subtle, but for me it has been the difference between the slow death of resignation and Life.

I have spent the afternoon leafing through old Bible study notebooks and prayer journals. My youthful passion for God's Word is organized by topics and books of the Bible. The pastor said it. I wrote it down. Roman numeral I, II, III, A, B, C. The flood of Bible teaching that poured from the pulpit caught in little pools of neatly printed paragraphs, some still wonderfully fresh with timeless insight, others clouded and stagnant with a subtle twist on the truth. A window on why I grew up with more of a passion for the facts of my faith than a Person to cherish:

From *Ecclesiastes*: "The only real happiness is in knowledge and application of Bible doctrine."

From *Daniel*: "God honors those who put doctrine first."

From *Acts*: On trial for his life Paul met "nothing but hostility and pressure, but Bible doctrine brought him through."

I wonder if Paul ever thought of it quite that way.

I am eternally grateful to my church and pastor for instilling in my life a firm foundation of God and his Word. Our church deeply honored the words God breathed into his chosen authors. We grieved over the public beating the Scriptures were taking from the culture and even from some churches. We gave sacrificially to foreign missionaries. We worshiped God in spirit and in *truth.* Today I read Frederick Buechner and other Christian authors who, in a world of great complexity and the hiddenness of God, struggle with doubt, and I wonder if part of what steadies my faith is that firm foundation from a brilliant scholar of the Word who taught with power and intellectual grit. Either that or I'm still too Blonde.

But as much as we loved God's Word as precept and proposition, somehow I missed the fullness of truth in John 1:1: "In the beginning was the Word, and the Word was with God, and the Word was God."

The truth was not just a proposition, but a Person. Maybe you've heard of the little girl whose Sunday school teacher asked, "What is brown, eats nuts, and has a bushy tail?" Her little hand shot up, but then she hesitated. "I want to say 'a squirrel,' but is it 'Jesus'?"

We could have used a little of her routine wisdom in our church where, instead of "Jesus," the answer to just about everything was "Bible doctrine." Our shepherds taught us to think about our faith less as a relationship and a little more like Driver's Ed: You learn the Bible facts in the lecture and make the right choices behind the wheel, and you'll be at rest, happy on your journey. Make the wrong choices, and you'll wind up a wreck in the ditch. If you find yourself in the ditch, apply the truth of 1 John 1:9 ("confess our sins"), and God's grace will haul you out of the ditch and get you back on the road. Sorrow for your sin is beside the point.

Propositions, principles, reasons, volition, transactions—we were children of the Enlightenment, far, far removed from our shameful cousins who literally installed a statue of the goddess of Reason in the Notre Dame Cathedral, but champions of their modern mind-set. It was all about the mind and the will. In our church and family we did not use God and passion in the same sentence. Our pastor cautioned us against projecting our emotions onto God, teaching us that God didn't have emotions like we did—part of his "otherness." Growing up, I imagined God to be rather patrician and nice, like presidential candidate John Kerry before Bill Clinton taught him how to loosen up. I didn't grow up thinking that God was passionate about me. I didn't hear others talk of being passionate about God. God's love for us and our love for God were reduced to sheer choice, an act of the will. Tenderness, longing, passion? I have some notes on "sentimentalism" I could show you.

From *Ephesians*: "Walk in love. Live a life controlled by love, *not maudlin and gushy*, but Christlike love—pursuing the will of God, obedient to the Father, self-sacrificing."

"Love has many faces, my Lord," said Guinevere. *"If you have my will, then you have the best of it."*

"Do I?" cried Arthur. *"Do I?"*

When I met Jack, he was a full-time seminary student working thirty hours a week and superintending a junior high department at a large church. To keep all those plates spinning, it took every ounce of discipline he could muster and a mentality he celebrated with a sign on his desk: "Do what needs to be done. When it needs to be done. Whether you like it or not."

It is a dream to be married to someone like this. It's like having a thoroughbred racehorse for a husband—one light touch on the reins of Scripture or reason, and he changes out of the wrong lane into the right lane. With me the Holy Spirit has to saw on the reins until I'm frothing at the bit, and sometimes he still has to get off and threaten me with a big stick. Which is why just "doing your duty" never completely did it for me. I am way too passionate about my own ideas.

Jack sensed my frustration and resignation and would try to encourage me, telling me we just need to "do our duty." And I would respond, "You just don't understand. I wish it were enough, but something's missing." And we would have these long talks about doing the right thing, making your choice, and I knew I should, and I tried, but, well, you've read my sorry progress. God has taught me something of who he is through suffering and obedience. But, given my history, the way I'm wired, and my divided heart, I needed a clearer vision of God's heart—to see what's in his face when he looks on me.

God grows our vision for him and his kingdom through the vision of other people he brings into our lives.

Not long after my watermark decision for obedience, Jack and I attended a conference together in Dallas. One of my favorite speakers rose to the podium. If anyone can inspire the troops to take the hill, it is Chuck Colson. We were the Christian marines on the frontlines of life, and he was waving the flag and moving even stubborn recruits like me to swell with kingdom pride and *do our duty* out of gratitude and honor to God.

In the next session this fellow we'd never heard of took the podium. The first words out of his mouth were something to the effect of, "With great respect for Mr. Colson I wish to disagree." Jack and I looked at each other. Who was this slight, happily energetic unknown to take on Chuck Colson? It was like Martin Short challenging Charlton Heston for the role of Moses.

This was our introduction to John Piper, whose topic was taken from his then newly released book *Desiring God*: "'Delight yourself in the

Lord!' (Ps. 37:4). 'Be glad in the Lord and rejoice!' (Ps. 32: 11). . . . How shall we honor God in worship? By saying, 'it's my duty'? Or by saying, 'it's my joy'?"[15] "Strong affections for God rooted in truth are the bone and marrow of biblical worship."[16] A scholar with a passion for God's Word was proposing that the love that most honors God is not sheer choice or just doing our duty. My tired, dutiful little heart beat faster.

Piper offered an illustration so simple; we marveled that we had never understood it before.

> Suppose on (my wedding anniversary) I bring home a dozen long-stemmed red roses for (my wife). When she meets me at the door, I hold out the roses, and she says, "Oh, Johnny, they're beautiful, thank you," and gives me a big hug. Then suppose I hold up my hands and say matter-of-factly, "Don't mention it; it's my duty." . . . Dutiful roses are a contradiction in terms. If I am not moved by a spontaneous affection for her as a person, the roses do not honor her. In fact they belittle her. They are a very thin covering for the fact that she does not have the worth or beauty in my eyes to kindle affection.[17]
>
> Truth without emotion produces dead orthodoxy. . . . On the other hand, emotion without truth produces empty frenzy and cultivates shallow people who refuse the discipline of rigorous thought. But true worship comes from people who are deeply emotional and love deep and sound doctrine.[18]
>
> For many, Christianity has become the grinding out of general doctrinal laws from collections of biblical facts. But childlike wonder and awe have died. The scenery and poetry and music of the majesty of God has dried up like a forgotten peach in the back of the refrigerator.[19]

Had he been in my old church? Had he seen my notebooks? I recently asked my father, "Dad, if loving God with all your heart means loving God with obedience *and passion,* how could we have missed the main thing—the greatest commandment?"

My dad responded, "Well, no one ever showed us that is what it meant." Such a simple and yet profound statement. God's Word clearly told us, but we didn't have the imagination to see what it looked like and what it meant for us.

It is hard to describe what it feels like for someone to put words to the empty place in your heart that has been longing for something it cannot express as long as you can remember. For even though God has made me a very passionate person, that passion was never directed or invited toward God in a way that reached my heart. Somehow I absorbed the idea that if you wanted to hook up a little passion caboose behind your engine of the will fueled by your coal car of reason and doctrine, well, fine. But you would probably run faster without it.

I left the church of my youth in my junior year of high school. A new Young Life high school ministry was beginning in our area. In their small group Bible study I discovered the love chapter, 1 Corinthians 13, the importance of the ministry and gifting of the body of Christ, and a few other things I think my church forgot to tell me. The old mechanical application of Bible doctrine gave way to a clearer vision of *relationship* with God. You don't just sin and fall in the ditch and call the 1 John 1:9 tow truck. Sin is that "giving of yourself" to another lover. If I acknowledge my sin to God, that may be the bottom line of confession. But if I don't feel the least bit of regret or sorrow, it is a measure of how little real affection I must have for God.

Although it was slow going, God's Spirit was chipping away the old image little by little. Through Piper's words God shattered another icon. I saw in John Piper's heart and eyes and words a passion for a God of passion who was greatly honored by our desire for him—a God who wanted my affection much more than my resignation.

You may have come from churches where your shepherds served neither dried peaches of orthodoxy nor the empty frenzy of all passion and precious little truth. You are welcome to skip this short rant and move on. Or you may read this and think it is indeed "maudlin and gushy." Didn't I just quote Jesus saying that the real proof of love is obedience? Yes, it's true. But does the *bottom line* of "dutiful roses" honor God like the *fullness* of "roses *and* affection"?

Who better knew the difference than David? God gave King David the highest title to which we can inspire: "A man after my own heart." If I look at David, I can see a heart that God loves, a reflection of God's heart. Frankly it's "gushy" and desperate and awestruck. In David's own words:

My heart shall rejoice in your salvation. (Ps. 13:5)

The voice of the Lord *twists the oaks and strips the forests bare. And in his temple all cry, "Glory!" (Ps. 29:9* NIV*)*

Oh, magnify the Lord *with me. . . . Those who look to him are radiant. (Ps. 34:3, 5)*

How precious is your steadfast love, O God! The children of mankind take refuge in the shadow of your wings. They feast on the abundance of your house, and you give them drink from the river of your delights. For with you is the fountain of life; in your light do we see light. (Ps. 36:7-9)

Radiant, rejoicing, crying out, "Glory!" feasting, drinking from a river of delights. . . . Was that a picture of my heart's response to God? At least sometimes?

I think the last time I cried, "Glory!" was in the flush of a 75-per-cent-off sale at Dillard's.

David's heart delights in the principles and precepts of God's Word. But he was a man who could spend his entire Saturday sitting in God's sanctuary just drinking in the fair beauty of his presence. His was the heart of a poet filled with imagination and obedience, a heart very much like the heart of Jesus. Yes, it's true that Christ's love was expressed in "pursuing the will of God, obedience to the Father, and self-sacrifice." But how can we look at Jesus' sacrifice and not see the depth of his passionate love for us? Why do we look at so many paintings and movies and see what Philip Yancey calls a "Prozac Jesus"?

In Yancey's book *The Jesus I Never Knew*, I found another sledge-hammer at work on my image of Christ:

The gospels reveal a range of Jesus' emotional responses: sudden sympathy for a person with leprosy, exuberance over his disciples' successes, a blast of anger at wholehearted legalists, grief over an unreceptive city, and then those awful cries of anguish in Gethsemane and on the cross.[20]

He seemed excitable, impulsively "moved with compassion" or "filled with pity." . . . Three times, at least, he cried in front of his disciples.[21]

Obstinacy frustrated him, self-righteousness infuriated him, simple faith thrilled him. Indeed, he seemed more emotional and spontaneous than the average person, not less. More passionate, not less.[22]

In a one-two-three punch, about the time I was catching Piper's and Yancey's fresh visions of God, along came another fellow with a sledgehammer. I was writing *Worldproofing Your Kids*, and I occasionally discussed my ideas with a friend, John Eldredge, who taught worldview at Focus on the Family Institute. He offered comments on my manuscript and helped me further by sending along a manuscript he was working on. The book was entitled *The Sacred Romance*. For someone who had grown up with God as a six-star general, that book was quite a shock.

The pastor of my youth had regularly groaned from the pulpit over all the pale, skinny Jesuses that saturated our cultural imagination. "Where is the Jesus that sawed thick planks of wood and toppled tables heavy with silver?" he would ask. The God who shone on the early screen of my imagination was, above all, powerful and smart. He had a great deal to teach me, and I was eager to learn. His strength exploded on the screen of my imagination in brilliant miracles of creation, drowning armies, and raising the dead. Later, in the burning inflammation of my joints, I felt the full weight of his sovereignty. But all that size and strength and unquestionable control kind of crowded out the love, I think. *Jesus as lover?*

From my early vantage point in our community of faith, it seemed we applauded strength and beauty and intelligence more than we delighted in bending down, coming near to a struggler, and lavishing grace and forgiveness. In my prayer journal I wrote: "May I really delight myself in you, God"; and then in the same breath, "Will you give me the desires of my heart if I trust in you?" Looking back, I think I may have been tap dancing in hopes that God would toss a few coins my direction. After the onset of my illness, I found myself still trying to shuffle a little soft shoe, trusting God had a purpose in the pain he allowed into my life. But here's the rub: When you are performing for someone, it's hard to get close. When you've been wounded by someone, even if intellectually you know it's for a purpose, it's difficult to draw near.

John echoed my thoughts in his manuscript: If we think of God as the Author behind the larger story of life, his intelligence and strength may have created the story, but they also separate us from him. "Power and knowledge don't qualify for heart. Indeed the worst sort of villain is the kind who executes his plans with cold and calculated precision. He is detached; he has no heart. If we picture God as the master-mind behind the story—calling the shots while we, like Job, endure calamity—we can't help but feel . . . (like) 'rats in the cosmic laboratory.'"[23] We wonder, where is his heart?

"What if," John asked, "just what if we saw God not as Author . . . but as the central character in the drama?"[24] Beginning with the "heroic intimacy" of the Trinity in eternity past, he retold the story with God as the hero, giving life, love, and the splendor of good gifts. When the hero was betrayed, first by the angels, then by Adam's race, John invited me into the grief and longing of God's heart at the loss of his beloved. He showed how God responded time and again with grace and lavish love. He deeply desires us and promises to come for us. God, as the Sacred Romancer, relentlessly pursues us . . . for what?

For our hearts—"our laughter, our tears, our dreams, our fears, our heart of hearts."[25] Not hearts as in emotions, but as in the biblical picture of heart—our deepest, truest selves.

It was as if John gathered together all my conflicted but still-trying-to-be-nice Christian feelings about God and packed them into words that bristled with razor-sharp spikes and hurled them right at God. And while I was waiting for God to strike us both with the plague, he took out his sledgehammer and smashed God. Only it wasn't really God, but just another faulty image, and the thing flew apart. And standing there was the Lover I've always longed for but didn't know how to find. But it didn't matter because he sent out his servants, and they found me shopping at Dillard's and *compelled* me to come to the banquet. Through all the suffering and halting steps of obedience, his Spirit had my heart all tidied up and ready to go. And finally I stood before him rejoicing, drinking in the delight of his presence.

"Glory," I whispered.

<hr>

I've always known that God loves me. But I guess it felt like the kindly love of a teacher for a student or the love of a strict disciplinarian father for his child. John Piper helped me see that *God longs to be worshiped with passion.* Philip Yancey helped me see that *God is more passionate than I ever imagined.* And John Eldredge helped me see that *God is more passionate for me.*

I've asked many people, "How did God move your heart from one of duty to one of delight?" A common response is, "I saw someone whose heart delighted in God, and I told God, 'I want what she has.'" When we want God like that, when we seek him with all of our hearts, it's an invitation. And God promises to show up.

It only makes sense to seek out people like that, to get next to them in real life or find a quiet corner with their books. But God is not waiting around. Look for the light and heat of his Spirit enlarging your heart and the screen of your imagination in the pain he allows and the choices he gives. Long ago he sent out his servants to beat the bushes for you. To me he sent a pastor loaded with Bible doctrine, the Young Life party throwing confetti and blowing their kazoos, and a string of thoughtful literary writers. Where would I be without them? Through the power of God's Spirit each had great impact or wrought drastic changes in my image of God. These were the ones with sledgehammers, but there were many others who chipped here and sanded there—Francis Schaeffer, Chuck Colson, Larry Crabb, Eugene Peterson, my parents, Grandmother Graham, the Freys, the Whitelocks, Joe Wall, S. Lewis Johnson, Lindsey O'Connor, Carol Kent, and Jack—to name just a few.

And the amazing thing is, most often I didn't seek what they brought me. Sometimes I was moving in their general direction; sometimes I was just out in the byways. They found me and invited me to the banquet.

God knows you're out there shopping at Dillard's or reading a book. He knows how his image plays on the screen of your imagination. He sees where you've pictured him a little too much like a bull-dozing General Patton or a kind, but unassertive Clark Kent. Or maybe you see him in fuzzy gray tones instead of living Technicolor. He wants you to see him in all his glory. He longs to give you his greatest blessings. He will allow seasons of suffering and send his servants with sledgehammers. They will smash your image of God. They will help you see his face. They will drag you to the banquet.

Isn't that where you want to be? Is it enough to live a nice Christian

life? Is it enough to choose obedience when your heart is stuck in resignation? You may be thinking you have given God the best of it.

"*I choose you.*"

"*Your will chooses me! Your heart chooses him.*"

"*Then you have the best of it. My will is stronger than my heart. Do
you think I put so high a price on my feelings? Feelings live for a moment
and the moment passes. My will holds me steady to my course through life.*"

"*As mine does me. And yet, all I have to do is look at you, and everything I believed in fades to nothing. All I want is your love.*"

"*You have it.*"

"*Do I? Do I? Then look on me as you looked on him.*"

What does Jesus see when we look on him? Does he see anything
like the reflection of his desire for us?

I caught that reflection recently in a wedding where the bride and
groom filled the sanctuary with the purity of their patience and the
high voltage of their anticipation. In the flickering of a hundred votive
candles and the profusion of cinnamon red and white roses, God's living picture of what he wants for me dazzled me to the brink of tears.
It didn't help that the groom's cheeks glistened as his bride approached
to the spare stringed accompaniment of "Amazing Grace." Or that she
gently wiped his tears as she took her place beside him.

Actually the moment came, not during the ceremony, but as I
ducked out just ahead of the crowd to attend another function. I
crossed the empty lobby just as the bride and groom burst in. He swept
her into his arms and turned a full circle, eyes locked, a passionate kiss.
Breathless, they clung to each other, drawing back to look at one
another and hugging again. No words other than "oh," "oh!" as in "Oh,
I can't believe it's finally true. I can't believe you're finally mine." It was
the way he looked on her and she looked on him. Their eyes showed
me again why God created me, why he endured the cross, despising the
shame, why he still pursues me and invites me to his wedding banquet:
He did it, he does it for passionate joy.

*As a bridegroom rejoices over his bride,
so will your God rejoice over you.* (Isa. 62:5 NIV)

9

LIFE:
THE STORY

*For when we were born, we were born into the midst of a great story
begun before the dawn of time.
A story of adventure, of risk and loss, heroism . . . and betrayal.
A story where good is warring against evil,
danger lurks around every corner, and glorious deeds wait to be done.*
JOHN ELDREDGE, *EPIC*

When I began thinking about God as my Lover and Life as his
Kingdom Story, the back of the wardrobe fell away. I felt like the
children who pushed aside the overcoats, stepped into C. S. Lewis's
enchanted kingdom of Narnia, and found themselves in the midst of
something large and dangerous.

Until I entered the wardrobe, I had thought of life as the next thing
+ everything else on my calendar. Life was Time. A progression through
the entries in my calendar notebook. I went to church on Sundays and
Bible study on Tuesdays, answered study questions MWF, taught college classes TTH. My faith was a relationship (of more obedience than
intimacy) + a system of beliefs. The doctrines in my notebooks. A
Christian worldview—all the precepts and principles and propositional
truth that answered our biggest questions about life.

The thing about a system of beliefs is, it gives you a window on the way the world works.

The thing about a story is, it invites you to participate in that world.

When I began to imagine life as living in a Kingdom Story, I began to think of the role I was called to live instead of thinking of life as the things that I do—showing up doctor's appointments here and soccer practice there. I began to wake up thinking about my role, not just as a servant, but, as my friend Leighton has put it, a "Redemptress." What is the most strategic way I can live my role today? At the doctor's office, at soccer practice? How can I be an encourager, show mercy, give more than words? I go out looking for the ways God is always at work, and I began to imagine life as a supporting player rather than the star.

"I am the Alpha and Omega." God tells us that the Story of Life is all about him.

And we might all agree in theory. Yes, Jesus holds everything together.

However, "It's all about me" is so ingrained in our culture, in our hearts. On the cover of a birthday card from my friend Patty, a cool-looking dude with a ponytail and a latte says:

"Happy birthday to you, happy birthday to you . . ."

Inside it reads, "It always has to be about you."

We laugh. In our best moments we affirm the truth, "It's all about God," but, oh, how we live that Hallmark card.

What does it mean for God to be "the author of life"? If God is an author and he could have written any story he wanted, what has he written? Let's step outside the universe for a moment, just outside the wardrobe, and imagine . . .

Imagine the Father enjoying Life to the full with the Son and the Spirit from all eternity. He needs our worship like a rose needs incense. God, if you really are all this glory—the sum of all beauty and goodness, wisdom and love, power and justice, and infinitely more than words can ever describe or our tiny minds can ever grasp—what do you want? Or to put it as John Piper does, if you are a living treasure, what is the greatest thing you could do?

Give yourself as a gift to others.

Picture a shower of diamonds falling into empty, uplifted hands.

However, Lord, if you are such an infinite treasure, how do you give yourself as a gift to finite creatures? If God is, as Frederick Buechner has said, that mystery of such intense power and glory that if we were to see him "head on" rather than in glimpses, we might be annihilated, how do we receive a gift that is so overwhelming?

It's like asking, "How do we hug the sky?"

We think, *Okay, if I could just see God, I would get him right.* No more need for sledgehammers or image-bashing. It would satisfy my longing. It would be the rocket ride beyond my frustration and loneliness. It would truly be "the answer." But from all accounts, seeing him face to face isn't enough. Or better said, it's too much. Remember all the people dropping and keeling over? How do we receive the gift?

God *tells* me what he's like in his Word. "He parted the heavens and came down; dark clouds were under his feet. He mounted the cherubim and flew; he soared on the wings of the wind. . . . Out of the brightness of his presence clouds advanced, with hailstones and bolts of lightning" (Ps. 18:9-12 NIV).

But the telling only goes so far. Imagine if there were no flood, no exodus, no David killing Goliath, no destruction of Jerusalem, no shepherds or wise men, no Calvary, no fulfillment of his promises, no changed lives, *no trace of God in action* in the past or the present. Our picture of God would be such a pale reflection of his glory.

In his book *Things Unseen*, Mark Buchanan passes on an analogy from Daniel Brown, author and pastor, who helps us understand how God wants to give himself to us as a gift:

> He could show us, he says, a photograph of his friends, and you'd literally see what they look like. And yet you'd still know almost nothing about them: their quirks, their virtues, the way they move, the timbre and inflection of their voices, their ways with others. A mere physical representation of people is perhaps the least interesting and least informative thing about them. The deeper things about friends are grasped by something other than sight.[26]

Isn't that true? You can *look* at my friend Vivian's picture and see her bright eyes and merry smile and perhaps guess what a delight she is. I can take things a step further and *tell* you about Vivian. I can tell you that she is the Miss Congeniality of our church. When it's time to sign up for our women's retreat, everyone wants to room with her. She has a walk-in heart, big enough to take in everyone and all their baggage, and a sense of humor that softens every jagged edge and, once it gets rolling, can take the entire room on a runaway ride that leaves you panting with aching sides at the finish.

You can see Vivian's picture, and I can even tell you what sort of a person she is. But the only way to discover what a treasure she is would be to seek out her company and let her show you who she really is in the story of everyday life.

I have come to realize that God doesn't want to merely *tell* us who he is; he wants to *show* us his heart in his Story of Life. The best stories always show, not just tell. In Acts 17:24-26 Paul stands with us outside the universe and tells us the point of God's Story: "The God who made the world and everything in it, being Lord of heaven and earth . . . made from one man every nation of mankind to live on all the face of the earth. . . ."

Okay, here's the part where we learn the main character's motivation, the purpose of his Story. God did this so that " . . . they should *seek God*, in the hope that they might feel their way toward him and find him. Yet he is actually not far from each one of us" (v. 27, emphasis mine).

Seek is one of those words we breeze by in Scripture because we know it too well. It's a dynamic word full of energy: "to go in search or quest of."

God's Story and Godsight are about "seeking." We don't find the word *relationship* in some versions of the Bible. His invitation to intimacy sounds like, "Seek me and live," " Seek my face," "Turn to me," "Call upon me," "Come to me," "Come near"—the very things we do when we are crazy about someone and we *want* them. Did you ever stake out a spot where you knew your path would cross with a certain someone and then look up in feigned surprise: "Well, hello, what are *you* doing here?" When we want someone we find very creative ways to seek the person out.

God authored a Story so that we could seek him, and he could give himself to us in the unfolding drama of life. Here is the source of the best sex, the most delicious banquet, the most precious jewels, the most gorgeous vistas, the most exciting adventures, and he longs to be enjoyed.

So why is he hiding?

You'd think if God really wanted intimacy with us, we wouldn't have to seek him quite so hard. Sometimes the hiddenness of God breaks my heart. *God, why are you hiding when we need you so?* My experience as the big parent of a small child has given me a glimmer of insight.

We've all seen them. The parents that dote on their daughter ad nauseam, dress her in $200 embroidered sweat suits, chauffeur her and her friends to endless play dates where they watch Lizzy McGuire videos on eighty-inch plasma TV's and play Dance Revolution Extreme video games till they collapse on their electronic mats. The pantry is always stocked with Puff Cheetos, Zebra Cakes, and Pop Tarts. Mom does all her laundry, cleans her room for her. Dad does all her chores for her, rescues her whenever she is in trouble, solves all her problems.

What happens? Does the child grow up to be a good friend and a team player?

We all know the answer. She launches one of those endless, forced wailing jags on the airplane because her parents forgot to put her Shopping Spree Barbie in her backpack, and when the flight attendant stops by, the parents shake their heads and mourn, "We just can't do anything with her." A few years later they can't even talk to her because she will start text messaging how horrible life is to her equally whiney friends while giving her parents the famous teenage eye roll.

As parents, we learn to hide ourselves sometimes. We hear the siren call of our toddler fretting and crying in the nursery, but we lash ourselves to the chair around the corner and refrain from swooping in to hold him. We don't offer to do all the homework or buy all the goodies. We help our children look things up in the encyclopedia or structure their college financial aid so that they have to find a job. We want to help them grow strong in character, become all they can be. And along the way, Lord willing, perhaps they do. And along the way perhaps they come to really see and value us more than if we run their forgotten lunch up to school three times a week.

And that, I think, is a tiny glimpse of why God isn't obvious. He does not want me to grow up to be like Paris Hilton.

Once I really began to imagine God writing his Story, it was like looking through the proper end of the kaleidoscope. Colors and patterns came into focus. God invites us out of our small stories "all about us" into an epic Story with a huge cast of characters—nations of men and women to inhabit the whole earth and seek him and find him.

To fully imagine the Story, look back with me, before America, before civilization, before Adam and Eve, before earth, before light. Picture the explosion of space and time in reverse, imploding into itself, receding into whatever "banged" to begin with, until even the first waves and quarks vanish into nothing. Look back before empty air or space until there was only God, planning how to give himself as a gift. The author of life was plotting out his Story, imagining the best way to create not the most perfect world, but the world that would best lead us to his heart. Picture the Creator in full creation mode.

"In the beginning, God . . ." Of course! Every good story starts with a character. Oh, there are some action movies loaded with special effects where the characters sort of get lost in the big-bang, big-burn razzle-dazzle. But the stories that capture our hearts are driven by characters.

Picture a cast to be created "in his image" so we can connect with him. So our mind can reason with his. So our desire for beauty can be overwhelmed by his. So our longing for love will lead us to straight to his heart. When my connecting points are unconnected, I feel it—all these deep longings to seek him and find him.

Picture a cast of billions, and yet when he was sketching out his Story, he had you and me personally in mind for our unique roles. Ephesians 1 and Romans 8 tell us that in some mysterious way, God knew us "before the foundation of the world" and chose us. He had the pages of our days "written into his book."

If we were going to cast the Story, I wonder what all the players would look like. I could people a world with tribes of slightly Blonde, energetic, creative types. (And you might be ready to shut the door and get some serious work done.) God chose key roles for murderers and adulterers, traitors who would betray and persecute him, sleazy bureaucrats who would milk people for tax money to buy Dead Sea condos, and liars and dying thieves and whores. Unlike the ancient Greek dramas, no masks would be needed. A limping tap dancer with secret daydreams fits right in. Everybody does.

Once God was ready to create his characters, what were they to do? Stand about and talk? Occasionally look around for God? Pick flowers? What does every story need?

Hint: Every couple of weeks I meet with a group of "Women Who Read" to discuss a book. Just this week we met to discuss a *New York Times* bestseller, *The Tulip: The Story of a Flower That Has Made Men Mad*. The cover blurbs promised a story of "greed, desire, anguish and devotion." I still might have hesitated to read a story featuring a plant in the lead except that my artist friend Lesley has written a "loose legend" of the history of coffee, all about sultans and kings who were trying to horde it and wily rouges who were trying to steal it, and the story holds you in thrall to the last page.

When we met to discuss *The Tulip*, we were all completely frustrated. We had slogged through over 100 pages, and none of us wanted to continue. By unanimous vote we ditched it, a first in three years of reading books together.

"What was wrong with this book?" I asked.

"It had no story."

"What do you mean by 'no story'?"

"It had no plot!"

"What do you mean by 'no plot'?"

"It was just description, description, description. . . . The flowers looked like such and such, the people paid this much for them . . ."

"Well, it did describe some action. What was missing from the action?"

" . . . There was nothing to it. No struggle, no *conflict* . . ."

"Ah."

Christian novelist T. Davis Bunn has said that every story has a simple plot:

A guy climbs a tree.

Another guy comes along and throws rocks at the guy in the tree.

The guy in the tree comes down and crushes the guy throwing rocks. The end.

Every story needs a plot. Characters can't just endlessly pick flowers or describe them. In order to grow and thrive, the characters need a challenge. Tension. Conflict.

God's plotline is very simple: Creation. Fall. Redemption. And it is packed with challenge and tension.

Creation: In Genesis his Story of Life begins with incredible drama—probably even a bang! He spoke and made it so—creating light and life on command.

I have tried this occasionally. "Let there be dinner on the table. Slim thighs in the mirror." It's a little beyond my range.

"Let there be words on a page."

This works a little better, especially with my voice recognition software. And I can bear witness that there is great tension and drama involved in creation. Me vs. a blank page. I fight to get the pictures off the glowing screen of my imagination and packed into little black words on a white screen. You know the tension of creation—finding a new way to get fifteen things done when you only have time for eight, or inspiring your kids to actually clean their rooms.

I can't imagine the drama of watching God create the world. Of taking hot, molten this and ice-cold that and stirring it into such stunning beauty. From God's discussion with Job we can imagine him setting earth spinning on its invisible foundation of gravity, drawing boundaries for the sea, and the entire project taking shape like clay being pressed under a seal while the bleachers erupted in a roar of music and cheers. "The morning stars sang together and all the angels shouted for joy." Then into the Garden of Eden, the crown jewel of his creation, God placed Adam and Eve.

Surely it was even more beautiful than the Canadian Rockies, which are probably the most glorious slice of creation I've ever been privileged to see. As Jack and I drove through Banff National Park on our twenty-fifth anniversary trip, we listened to an audio tour of the mountains—the history, Indian folk legends, and always a little geology lesson: "A molten thrust here, a glacier grind there." All this stunning beauty is the product of chance. The random distribution of atoms. No design. No heart of beauty behind it.

Winding along the Bow River, taking in the sweeping vistas of icy peaks robed in luxuriant folds of lodge pole pine, I couldn't help but think of Isaiah 45:18 (NIV): "For this is what the LORD says—he who created the heavens, he is God; he who fashioned and made the earth, he founded it; he did not create it to be empty, but *formed it to be inhabited*—he says: 'I am the LORD, and there is no other.'"

God planned his characters, writing their names in his book.

Then he designed a *set to be inhabited* by these characters.

As opposed to Mars. Remember when the Mars rovers beamed back their pictures of the set design on the next planet over? I stared at the frozen, dusty, red barrenness stretched across the front page of the paper and couldn't help but think: *This is what the neighborhood looks like when it is* not *designed to be inhabited.*

Creation may well have started with a bang, but the more we discover it, the more the deep design astonishes us. There was nothing random about it. All the while he was creating, God was focused on the purpose of his Story: that we would find him and delight in what a treasure he is. We did not randomly evolve from the set. That would be putting the temporal cart before the eternal horse. We are the ones with eternal destinies. Our names were written in the Lamb's Book of Life "from the foundation of the world" while the elements will one day melt like burning wax. The set is designed for us to inhabit and find in it a million clues that point us back to God. I would venture a guess here: No great author starts with a set. You design the set to help your characters live out a revelation of truth and reality that resonates with the human heart.

The more we see of God's set, the more we see ultimate reality—his heart. "For since the creation of the world God's invisible qualities—his eternal power and divine nature—have been clearly seen, being understood from what has been made, so that men are without excuse" (Rom. 1:20 NIV).

These verses invite us to think of creation as God's home page.

The stars sermonize every night: "There is a God so big he could scatter us like diamonds. Then there is you." Creation gives us a proper sense of scale. From the viewpoint of what may be the only inhabited planet in the universe, the galaxies are not so much "wasted space" as some suggest. They measure the largeness of God.

Last summer I traveled to Orlando one weekend and Colorado the next. As I gained altitude and ever-grander vistas on the cog railway to the summit of Pike's Peak, what hit me was not culture shock, but creation shock. Shaking off the "all about you"-ness of Orlando's museums and thrill rides and five-star resorts and the universe's finest entertainment venues designed to thrill and enchant and cater to your every whim and, instead, feeling like a small speck on a gigantic mountain. Not that I am supposed to feel inconsequential and meaningless, but that I am to let the mountain take me to the greatness and majesty of God.

In God's set there is beauty for beauty's sake—because God wants us to be dazzled by his beauty. I remember back in my recreational era hiking to a remote mountain meadow where I was staggered by the sight of snowy peaks, an icy green lake, and a confetti of the most brilliant, delicate wildflowers. "Lord, all this beauty tucked away here when down in Houston we would kill for a few hills and a clear lake of any color?" God owns so much beauty he can squander it in places few ever see.

God's set not only shows us his size and beauty, but I think he invites us to look into his creation and see a world of metaphors designed to give us Godsight. "A metaphor is meant to describe a mystery," explains theologian Sarah Sumner. We use metaphors ("She's rubbing the fingernails of her ambition down the chalkboard of her limited ability") to paint a word picture using something that is better known to describe something else that is lesser known. And to do it with more power, more range, and a more direct connect to our hearts and imaginations than simple facts such as, "She's not very talented," can express.

While we reach for metaphors to explain the reality of someone's ability, I think God did it just the other way around. I think he created the seen world to give us handles on the hidden reality of his heart. "He did all this," made the cosmos and peoples and nations so we could "feel our way to him and find him."

Reread the psalm on page 117 and take away the "dark clouds," "the wind," "the hailstones and bolts of lightning," and try to convey God's dangerous power and majesty. Even the verbs take their meaning from creation. How could you picture him "mounting the cherubim" if you had never seen anyone mount an animal? How could you imagine "flying" or "soaring" if you had never seen a bird?

Long before there was a sunrise and a new day, there was a God who wanted to give us a picture of fresh beginnings—how his mercies are "new every morning."

Aeons before there was the exploding energy of spring, there was a God who planned to invite us into his resurrection life.

Long before there was a rainbow, there was a Technicolor God.

Think how Jesus used the pictures of creation. I wonder if God created sparrows so Jesus could point to something small and common and say, "If he cares about one of these falling to the ground, how much more does he care for you?"

Jesus said, "I am the Bread of Life and the *True* Vine. I am the *real* thing after which all these others were patterned."

Living in God's setting, we experience the heat and barrenness of a parched and thirsty desert and get a sense of our need for Living Water.

We feel the darkness of a long tunnel of night and long for the brightness of the Light of the World.

Even our relationships serve as metaphors to help us seek and find God's heart. We cradle a newborn child in our arms. Our hearts well up, and we understand how our Father feels about us. When our children waste our good advice and tender care, we feel his sorrow over our own prodigal moments and seasons.

God is so much more Life than I imagined. Again and again he uses his creation to *show* us his heart.

God is so much more purposeful than I imagined. He creates with a plan and rules with a reason. God crafted a setting that leads us at every turn to the Set Designer.

Peyto Lake is one of the most shockingly beautiful places on the planet. Maybe the universe. While Jack took a hike, I sat on the observation deck watching as visitors caught their first glimpse of the neon turquoise lake shimmering below. Eyes widened. Smiles shone. Orientals, Europeans, Hispanics—all responded to God's incredible artistry in the universal language of delight and amazement: "Ooo! Aaah! Oooh!"

Onto the deck walked a man, nicely dressed, in his sixties I guessed, with a retractable cane used by the blind. Slowly he tilted his head back, face to the sunny sky. My eyes teared up. *Oh*, I thought, *how awful to be blind in this stunningly beautiful place.* Twenty-two years with rheumatoid arthritis have sensitized my antennae to others with physical disabilities.

Head still back, he exclaimed to his wife, "Clear sky, hardly a cloud in it. These incredible mountains . . . this is a great day!"

Hmmm. My emotional gearbox ground into reverse. I scolded myself, *Okay, I'm the drama queen making up a tear-jerking scene here where there is none.*

But then the man's very attentive wife began describing a few things to him. "Oh, this lady has a little pug dog. Down there is another observation deck. I think I'll go down there and take a look." She walked off, and he sat down by me.

I tried to think of a nice way to ask, "Are you blind?"

I had come down a short trail from a special handicapped parking area; so I asked him, "Did you hike up the longer trail from the parking lot below?"

"No, I walked down the short one from handicapped parking. I'm blind. I can see dim outlines of things like the mountains and people, but four years ago my optic nerve suddenly degenerated."

I told him about my own physical limitations and how deeply I felt for him.

"Well, I've learned a lot," he replied. "I've become more patient and tender, and I've become a stronger Christian."

I discovered his name was David Winter, and he had been president of Westmont, a Christian college in California, for twenty-five years, the last three after he lost his sight. By God's grace and a daily choice to persevere in his work, he had indeed learned a great deal from his loss. Now he enjoyed a semi-retired role as chancellor. Our encounter led to sharing dinner with them and their traveling companions the next night. When I reflected back to him how his response on that deck, in spite of his loss, had touched me, his wife smiled. "That's David. He gets up every morning, throws back the curtains, and says, 'Isn't this a beautiful day!'"

Later I wrote him a note thanking him for his heart and quiet testimony. "I don't know what brought more glory to God," I wrote, "that turquoise lake rimmed by mountains or your heart of praise."

My question lingered long after I sent the letter. And as I've thought about it, I have an idea of the answer: The mountains' beauty pierces our hearts and gives us a glimpse of a Creator so majestic that only he could dream them up. But the mountains just stand there—doing what they're supposed to do. They cannot choose to do otherwise.

David lost his sight. He is more dependent now on his wife and others for the simplest of tasks. But this man who is blind to the brilliance of Peyto Lake stands on an observation deck and looks out with Godsight. He sees what is real. His joy springs from a heart that chooses to seek and delight in God in some very dark places. And while the mountains will wear out "like a garment" one day, David's heart and praise will last forever.

Which brings more glory to God?

I'm thinking David.

So is it any surprise that God put a choice into his perfect setting? He put Adam and Eve at Eden's equivalent of Peyto Lake and said, "You have me. You have all this beauty and high adventure. You have work to do—fill the earth and subdue it. Rule. Craft a language and dream up a love life. Grow things. Build things. Create families and culture. Teach your children. Enjoy work with challenge and without toil.

"And . . . you have a choice. You have all these trees to eat from. But don't eat from this tree." In the midst of all the good gifts God put up a small fence of protection.

God offered this incredible *invitation* loaded with freedom and promise. Imagine it. Dream it. Do it. The possibilities for intimacy and meaningful work and recreational adventure were limitless. Adam and Eve lived in a garden planted by God. If we can still catch glimpses of his breathtaking design distorted by time and catastrophe, how must it have been to live in it fresh? Straight from his hand and heart? Can you imagine what it must have been like to ask God your questions, hear about his work? Seek the guidance you need and savor the progress together?

Over the course of time though, something happened. Adam's and Eve's perspective changed. They looked past the *invitation* and could only see the *fence* . . .

10

FIERY STONES:
THE BACK-STORY

You sharpen the human appetite to the point
where it can split atoms with its desire;
you build egos the size of cathedrals;
fiber-optically connect the world to every eager impulse;
grease even the dullest dreams with these dollar-green,
gold-plated fantasies, until every human becomes an aspiring emperor,
becomes his own God. . . .
THE DEVIL AS JOHN MILTON, *THE DEVIL'S ADVOCATE*

Star Wars. Indiana Jones. Many of our best stories begin with a shiv-ering dramatic sequence. As the story unfolds, we catch glimpses or entire scenes from the back-story—what happened earlier, before this story begins—that help us better understand why the emperor is hunting Luke and his droids or why Indiana would take on the Nazis.

God began his Story, not with the fellowship of the Trinity, not with him on his throne in eternity past, but just like a Hollywood block-buster. We are dropped into the Story right in the middle of the action: God flinging stars into the blackness of space. He wants us to know: *I created you, and I offer you an invitation to Life.* But while that was the

beginning of *our part* of the Story, it was not the beginning of *the* Story.
Scripture is sprinkled with flashbacks, snapshots of life, and conflict
that happened before Genesis 1 began.

As I've begun to imagine Life as the Story God has written and live
my role with Godsight, I've caught a clearer vision of the tension and
conflict at the heart of the Story. What happened? Why are things in
such a mess? Understanding why we find ourselves in so much conflict helps me know how to respond. God has his invitation, his dreams
for us. But God has an enemy with dreams of his own. The tension at
the heart of the Story is not just the challenge of creating, building, and
ruling. It is also the conflict of war.

Imagine, if you can, what it would mean to be perhaps the most
perfect being God ever created. On a one to ten scale . . . an eleven.
Beautiful inside and out with a heart full of wisdom and a purity of
vision and motives that was a model for everyone else. To have the
power to speak your thoughts into another's mind, command the lightning and winds to obey your desires. Suppose you were all this beauty
and perfection and power, and you were unleashed to follow your
wildest dreams? What kind of role would you live in God's Story?

In Ezekiel 28 we are given a flashback into the angelic story before
ours, which introduces this character and, with him, the heart of the
conflict and tension in God's Story:

> *You were the model of perfection, full of wisdom and perfect in beauty.*
> *You were in Eden, the garden of God;*
> *every precious stone adorned you: ruby, topaz and emerald, chrysolite,*
> *   onyx and jasper, sapphire, turquoise and beryl.*
> *Your settings and mountings were made of gold;*
> *on the day you were created they were prepared.*
> *You were anointed as a guardian cherub, for so I ordained you.*
> *You were on the holy mount of God;*
> *   you walked among the fiery stones. (Ezek. 28:12-14 NIV)*

Around Oscar time we see the stars walk the red carpet in diamond
sandals, diamond beading on their gowns, and diamonds dripping

from their necks and arms. I read of a Saudi prince who ordered his suits pin-striped with twenty-four-carat gold thread. But they would pale beside Satan. Of all the angels gathered in joyful assembly, he dazzled on the mount paved with stones as fiery as his own appearance.

Imagine that assembly—the alien beautiful seraphs hovering above God's throne crying, "Holy, holy, holy"; the angel John sees in his prophetic Revelation (10:1), "robed in a cloud, with a rainbow above his head; his face was like the sun, and his legs were like fiery pillars"; the angel that appeared to Daniel as a man dressed in linen with a belt of the finest gold around his waist, a body "like chrysolite, his face like lightning, his eyes like flaming torches, his arms and legs like the gleam of burnished bronze, and his voice like the sound of a multitude." Imagine an assembly filled with these creatures stretching as far as the eyes can see and Satan the most splendid of all.

Imagine not just their beauty in assembly, but their power in action—how with a touch one strengthened Daniel, and without a touch or even a word another sprang Peter's chains and swung open the locked iron gate into the city. Another struck down 70,000 people with a lethal plague in judgment on King David's sin.

Ezekiel 28 goes on to say, "You were blameless in your ways from the day you were created till *wickedness was found in you.*"

A friend leaves his wife for a woman who makes him feel like he never really was loved before. A baby born with half a brain is held in his parents' arms, loved and named, only to die a few hours later. Another bombed-out vehicle in the Mideast takes a son from his mother. We reel in shock. We don't want to know. We want to draw into ourselves and retract our antenna that connects us to the painful heart signals of others. We can't help but wonder, *How did it come to this? How did this battle begin?*

The Bible gives us this oblique and mysterious answer: Sin was found in Satan.

We think it absolutely incredulous until a pattern that is wantonly familiar emerges: We're at the height of our personal glory—the contract is signed, our daughter is voted homecoming queen, our son stands at the altar, our ministry is praised . . . and suddenly it's all about us. *Aren't we wonderful?*

At the height of beauty and power and purity, Satan looked past the invitation to enjoy life at the pinnacle and instead swelled and took aim at what was fenced off. In this case, not just the Tree of the Knowledge of Good and Evil, but the very glory of God.

> *You said in your heart, "I will ascend to heaven;*
> *"I will raise my throne above the stars of God;*
> *"I will sit enthroned on the mount of assembly,*
> *on the utmost heights of the sacred mountain.*
> *"I will ascend above the tops of the clouds;*
> *"I will make myself like the Most High." (Isa. 14:13 NIV)*

It is a small step from the peak of beauty and power and wisdom . . . to pride. *What is Satan's passion? What dreams does he dream?* "I will ascend . . . I will ascend above the tops of the clouds, ascend all the way to heaven."

Satan's passion is to rise. "I will make myself like the Most High."

Satan's dream is to be up where God is and say, "I will take control, and I'll take what I want." Like Eve's dream, reaching out, perhaps a little hesitantly, just touching the fruit. Glancing around, searching the sky, encouraged by the lack of consequences. It is Eve firmly grasping the fruit, jerking it off the tree, and sinking her teeth into it, thinking, *Mmm . . . good move. I'll be as wise as God.*

Satan's dream is to take God's place. It is a declaration of a war that plunged all heaven into battle, a nuclear tsunami of angelic violence that only abated when Satan was cast out of heaven and a third of the angelic legions with him.

The war came to earth in a scene that looks so pastoral, so ordinary. A woman takes fruit from a tree and eats it. She offers it to her husband with a smile. They have no idea. Like the commercial where the man takes out his credit card and unleashes hordes of axe-wielding vandals coursing through the neighborhood or the stadium. Only the angels that fell from the joyful assembly don't just trample the grass and knock over benches. They afflict with disease and inspire men to murder and steal; they command lightning to strike and mighty desert winds to sweep in and tear down a house and turn a family reunion into a mass funeral. And that is just the report from one man's story in the book of Job.

Adam and Eve could not imagine what lay on the other side of that fence of protection. In my Cosmic Blonde Tap-Dancing years, I could not imagine it either. Even though I memorized Ephesians 6:10-18 to get a crown. We war "against powers, against the rulers of the darkness of this world, against spiritual wickedness in high places" (KJV). But the reality of war is incompatible to a Blonde frame of mind and an imagination full of tap-dancing dreams.

When we look at life with Godsight, we see it as . . .

. . . an invitation to seek and find God: "'Come!' Whoever is thirsty, let him come; and whoever wishes, let him take the free gift of the water of life" (Rev. 22:17).

. . . an invitation to "Rule, build, subdue the earth."

And we expect to have to wage war to do it.

When we look at life with Godsight, the fence around enemy territory—options that are available but harmful—looks small. In fact, the fence of protection feels safe, holding back the chaos and danger so we can enjoy Life in the Story.

When our imagination is captive to the "evil enchantment of worldliness," we don't dream of finding the treasure of intimacy with God or winning a war. Our dreams of building and ruling can become dreams of rising—of building magnificent mud pies in the slums.

When I am dreaming dreams of rising, I look past God's invitation and start staring at the fence, and it starts to grow. It shoots up about fifteen feet, grows five rows of razor wire across the top, and comes closer and closer, wrapping itself around me, until the invitation all but disappears, and my heart dreams of escape.

Instead of seeing the invitation,

I see only the obligation.

Stay inside the fence. Don't open the gate.

And because I am a good Christian, I don't open the gate and grab all the fruit hanging low and luscious on the branches.

No, I sit down nicely inside the fence, quietly even, and let my imagination go winging right over the razor wire, grabbing one fruit and then another until the imaginary juice streams down my face and all over my clothes, and I am dirty and sticky, but still achingly hungry for fruit.

And God seems dangerously close to Peter Cook's caricature of him in the original 1967 movie of *Bedazzled*. In this updated version of Dr. Faustus' deal with the devil, Cook plays Lucifer tutoring his new soul under contract, Stanley Moon (Dudley Moore), in his perspective of how the universe really works. He is especially keen to set his new convert straight on the true nature of God. To cast the vision for Dudley, Cook perches, godlike, atop a postal box and says, "I'm God. This is my throne, see? All around me are the cherubim, seraphim, continually crying, 'Holy, holy, holy,' the angels, archangels, that sort of thing. Now you be me . . . sort of dance around, praising me."

"What do I say?"

"Anything that comes into your head that's nice—how beautiful I am, how wise I am, how handsome, that sort of thing. Come on, start dancing." The devil sits on the "throne" staring straight ahead, aloof, indifferent, urging Dudley to keep it up: "Make it more personal, a bit more fulsome. Please, come on . . ."

One full circle around the throne, and Moore is tired and bored and not a little resentful, which, as the Devil and Dudley see it, proves the Devil's point exactly: Who would want to serve someone who loves nothing more than to sit on his throne, an arrogant, self-absorbed egotist, and make all the people in heaven dance around and worship him, on and on and on, singing and bowing, world without end?

The scene grabbed me by the throat and shook me. Blasphemy! For a moment I understood why people ripped their clothes and sentenced offenders to die long, slow deaths on the rack. If you love God, or anyone, you want to rise up and launch the carriers when you see that loved one mocked and ridiculed so callously. I hated for anyone to think God was anything like that.

Looking back on it, I wonder if the real reason it rattled me lay at a deeper level. It raised the same question that hovered, unacknowledged, unanswered, in the air of my life inside the fence: *Are God's dreams of happiness and my dreams of happiness the same?* I saw the movie in my RA-onset, TV-sotted season when it really did seem like God's dreams of happiness inside the fence were holding me back, not inviting, and my dreams of happiness liked to sneak over the fence. It took a great deal of duty and resignation to let go of my dreams and try to be content with God's. *If my dreams seemed so different from God's dreams in this life, how would they become the same in heaven? Would God's idea of happiness change? I knew he never changes. Would my idea of happiness change? Why can't I want his happiness now?*

Everything comes down to Godsight. How do we see God? Who is God really? And what does he want? Is God really a rewarder or an egotist who likes an audience? And we can get to that point where our imagination seems to go to a picture-in-picture screen. On a larger part of the screen shines the truth of Revelation 22:12 (NIV): "I am coming soon! My reward is with me." He's the living treasure and the great rewarder. But down in the bottom right-hand corner are all those people dancing around the throne—dancing and bowing and getting really tired.

I do not like to confront this choice. I'd much rather imagine God as the rewarder in the distance and my dreams of rising as a gray area. But Jesus has laid my Cosmic Blonde Tap-Dancing dreams out on the table and asked me point blank, "Are your dreams more like mine or the enemy's?"

Isaiah tells us that, in fact, the Devil is the tap-dancing achiever who dreams of sitting enthroned while all the people in heaven worship *him*.

"I will ascend."

"I will make myself like the Most High."

"I will sit enthroned on the mount of assembly."

The passion of pride is to rise higher than those around you.

The heart of the enemy says straightforwardly, "I want the throne in the temple. *I want to be UP above everybody else.*" It is not enough to savor his own beauty and gifts and be rewarded and validated by God.

The heart of pride is competitive. It wants to be on the throne surrounded and admired by others who are compelled to look at it and notice how wonderful it is. And even dance and bow a little.

The very picture of God's "true nature" that the Devil so pointedly mocks in *Bedazzled* never entered God's mind. If God is a living treasure who wants to *give himself* as a gift to others, then surely the last thing he desires is the arrogantly exultant scene the Devil described. When we finally see God on his throne, we won't be able to keep ourselves from praising him. It will be sheer pleasure, so exciting that our hearts will race with joy. To imagine that scene the way that Peter Cook and Dudley Moore paint it would be to think that the bride walking down the aisle to her lover wants to yawn but is being compelled to smile. To think that your child has just been born, and you'd rather hand him off and turn on the soaps, but the nurse is making you hold him in your arms.

The irony is rich. The scene from *Bedazzled* is really a picture of Satan's own dreams, imagined by the ultimate tap dancer who longs to take the stage and *devour* everyone's applause and *give nothing* of himself in return. And he invites us to do the same. Sometimes his appeal is quite blatant, like when my dad wanted my mom to look at a swanky new RV. The moment she stepped inside, she said, "Get thee behind me, Satan." Usually he whispers much more seductively in our ear . . .

. . . as we watch our next-door neighbor drive by in her spanking new car. "You deserve it more than she does. Talk to your husband."

. . . as we listen to our brother delight in his son's award. "Your son deserves it more than his son does. All he needs is little push. Get on him."

. . . as we see our co-worker's picture in the company newsletter. "You could have done that. You're more talented than she is. Step it up this next year."

. . . as we sit in the Bible study discussion group. "Why does the entire conversation have to be about her and her kids? What about me? My kids?"

The enemy comes to us like John Travolta, flashing his baby blues, smiling slyly, and invites us to his big it-all-depends-on-you-because-God-can't-be-trusted tap dance. *Don't you want a body, a romance, a voice, a lifestyle? Grab it! Take the throne.*

And *when*, not *if*, our rising is thwarted, the enemy whispers in sympathy with our disappointments. *Oh, what a terrible waste. You have so much beauty and talent, and you were one of the best tap dancers ever. How could anyone with a heart inflict you with RA? You're handling it so well. You deserve your little escape.*

He comes to us like Diane Sawyer, so understanding, wanting our story, laughing at the right moments, blue eyes sparkling, blonde hair shining, tearing up at the right moments. Digging out our resentment and hurt in an unguarded moment. Inviting us to vent just a little for the camera.

When the enemy shows up like John Travolta or Diane Sawyer on the screen of our imaginations, we so desperately need a clearer vision of who he really is:

He is really Hannibal in his cell humming "I Did It My Way," plotting our rape and murder and how he will cook up our liver for dinner.

He is really the roaring lion on the *National Geographic* special, salivating over the prospect of devouring us. He wants to stalk us and chase us and take us down. He wants to sink his jaws into our jugular and rip our flesh off the bone and swallow us and lap up the pool of our blood.

And God is everything that is the opposite. He invites us to savor the banquet that he is. Think of the cross. Think of the symbolism of Communion. While the enemy wants to crush and devour us, God offers his flesh as the bread of life and his blood as the wine of the new covenant. He wants us to taste and see how good he is. Surely we can trust his heart and his invitation.

How do my dreams compare to Satan's dreams? To Jesus' dreams?

Satan's dream is rising.

Jesus' dream was just the opposite. His passion was to descend. What a contrast of imagery:

Satan's passion: Rising.

How high? Follow the landmarks of his ascent from Isaiah 14:

> From the tops of the clouds, up to heaven,
> up to a throne above the stars,
> up to make himself like God.

Jesus' passion: Descending—a trip down exactly the same scale! He begins where Satan aspires to go, that magnificent throne high and lifted up. He *is* God. But out of his great love for us he descends.

Follow the landmarks of his descent in Philippians 2:5:

> From the throne,
> to the appearance of a man,
> to a servant,

to die,

to the humiliation and agony of crucifixion.

He offered himself to be devoured by Satan and by our pride and greed that moves in the same direction. All that violent ripping and tearing and crushing he willingly embraced to protect us from the raging lion. We take our sin so casually, and he "cares about sin with a fiery passion," enough to embrace the cross, because he knows sin keeps us from seeking him—the very purpose for which we were created. The whole point of the Story and the universe and everything else.

And I have to ask myself, *In which direction does my passion move? What are my dreams?*

Rising or descending?

What do I delight in thinking about? Which theme characterizes my conversation? Where is my energy directed? How do I plan my days? How do I spend my money, rising or descending?

My best answer is "both"; my heart moves in both directions. Please don't ask me for any statistics.

I have a lot of rising built into my heart.

And a long history of it from childhood.

Furthermore, I am American; therefore, I rise.

Rising is a huge part of who we are as Americans. Our forefathers' quest to build the City on the Hill for the glory of God has devolved into what David Brooks calls the "Paradise Spell," our limitless imagination for a future of Better Homes, Better Schools, Better Cars for the sake of Progress, Comfort, and Happiness, which has further devolved into A Million and One ways to tap dance and shop Sam's for things we don't need, but got such a great deal on. . . .

And it's very difficult to discern where my descending ends and my rising begins. Especially since we've been given the invitation to rule and subdue, grow and build. At the heart of God's Story of Life is an invitation to a holy kind of rising. Paul tells the churches, "Whatever you do, work heartily, as for the Lord and not for men" (Col. 3:23); "I press on toward the goal for the prize of the upward call of God in Christ Jesus" (Phil. 3:14). My new heart is rightfully discontent with mediocrity and a fractured creation that groans until Jesus comes to make it right. It pulses with a creative energy to live my role as God's Kingdom Redemptress.

Much of the rising in my imagination is holy rising: loving a family, building relationships, a church, a home that welcomes others, doing work that will count for more than my own satisfaction and kudos from my friends. The difference between holy rising and Satan's rising is, Who gets to be seated in the assembly? Who gets the applause? Do I want it for God or myself? The true test of this is hiddenness. Am I willing to serve when the applause comes only from him or is offered to him and others? On the hidden screen of my imagination, do I dream of applause for God or for myself?

As an author, when you first get published, you're just grateful to be "in the club," as my friend Lindsey and I have teased each other. Where you go from there is a real test of your heart. I walked the floor of the big annual publishing convention one summer and found myself thinking:

Don't they want to promote my book as much as hers?

Why is the publisher's rep walking with her arm around her? Why, when she's walking with me, is she talking on her cell phone?

I remind myself of a comment I once heard radio host Roger Gray make about pet psychologists: "Pet psychologists, what is that? You pay fifty bucks an hour for someone to tell you what your dog is really saying when he's out in the yard barking? I'll tell you what he's saying. He just wants attention. He's saying, "Hey, hey, hey, hey-hey!""

That's my lowest-common-denominator rising self. "Hey, hey-hey, hey . . . I just want attention . . . hey, hey." I catch myself comparing and yipping for attention. *Stop noticing her and notice me.*

In *The Divine Embrace*, Ken Gire challenges those of us who long to give full expression to our expansive imaginations: "As a creative person, it is humbling to acknowledge this, but the Scriptures place little value on our need to express ourselves in unique and original ways. . . . At the core of the temptation is the deception that what matters more than anything else in life is expressing our ideas, achieving our goals, actualizing our dreams."[27]

My challenge is, do I want God's dreams and purposes far above my own? Do I want others to look at me and see Jesus Christ and celebrate him? Do I want my work to be a means of descending to serve other people, or do I mostly work out of some sense of, *Ah, this is what I'm good at?* Or because I long for praise—a zippy ten-star review in *Publisher's Weekly?*

Thinking back on my season of flights of fantasy and daydreaming, early on it seemed like such a harmless, gray area. *Okay, God, my fence is so big and my possibilities for life are so much smaller than I had hoped. Surely you wouldn't begrudge me my mental recreation, my twenty to twenty-five hours in front of the tube. And here in my little fenced yard I'm living for you, doing what ministry I can, taking care of my family. It's not like it's an addiction. It doesn't control me. It's not the center of my life. Just a harmless diversion as I'm driving or washing dishes or taking a short rest or going to sleep at night, just a creative alternative to counting sheep.*

I wish during that season I had been able to sit down with myself and ask a few questions of my heart:

Lael, what about this rising thing?

How do your dreams compare to the dreams of the enemy?

Do you weave a story to satisfy your need for attention? Do you dream of being a Redemptress, part of a community, laughing and loving together, serving one another? Or is the focus on you being "enthroned in the assembly," the heroine who receives the praise for herself?

Do you dream of being high and lifted up or reflecting the slightest praise and glory back to the one who has given you the time and gifts and measure of health to do something worthy of praise? When you rewrite the plotline of your life, even in your head, is it a subtle way for you to take control and be like God?

If we watch TV and movies and imagine ourselves into those plotlines, or imagine the celebrities we like into our plotlines, is it a harmless pastime? Is it as much about rising and control as when others act out their longings with real plotlines and partners? Is it different from the *kind* of thing my friend's mom chose when she ditched her family and flew off to Atlanta to meet her "you've got mail" soul mate? Or is it only different in *degree?* Is it neutral, as long as we keep it all blazing on the screen of the imagination?

We shrink back, defending ourselves—*I would never cross the line and act anything out.*

But, because these things are secret, and we don't want to share them with anyone, it's good to keep probing, asking questions. How could romantic fantasy or pornography keep us from finding the life we long for?

What about rest and recreation? Do our flights of imagination into books, movies, Big Bucks for Bizarre hobbies, regular hobbies, Web browsing, casual e-mail, or Web chat restore and redirect us back into the life of spending ourselves for the kingdom, or does it work the other way around? Are we constantly looking for opportunities to get back to the fantasy plotline or the chat room or the book or the new home improvement project? Not just an occasional detour or refreshing sideline as much as a pattern of living that pulls us away from relationships and ministry?

How do our dreams of treasures here stifle our investment in rewards that last forever?

For any of us seeking the life we long for in our own imaginations, or someone else's imaginations on a real TV or movie screen, or even one step removed in the virtual but private world of cyberspace, how do our imaginary or virtual adventures keep us from engaging in real ones?

Do you ever hear God's Spirit floating a few of these questions your way? What do our worldly dreams and fantasies cost us?

May I say this ever so gently but earnestly from one who has tap-danced and longed and grieved and imagined and wrestled with these questions . . .

There is a price for living small.

11

KILLING US
SOFTLY

The dilemma of the Story is this:
We don't know if we want to be rescued.
We are so enamored with our small stories and our false gods,
we are so bound up in our addictions . . . and our
take-it-for-granted unbelief
that we don't even know how to cry out for help.
JOHN ELDREDGE, *EPIC*

It is sunrise in *The City of Angels*, both the city and the movie. The guardian angels, their long black trench coats softly flapping in the Pacific breezes, gather silently in irregular formation along the beach. Gazing into and even beyond the sun, their eyes see into eternity. Their ears hear heaven's song. The vision transports and connects them to that reality beyond the grasp of our imagination. After sunrise they disperse, resuming their vigilant posts at hospitals, airports, and perched atop the downtown skyscrapers.

As the story unfolds, an angel, *Seth* (Nicholas Cage), becomes deeply attracted to a heart surgeon, *Maggie* (Meg Ryan). He hovers near her in the hospital stairwell where she weeps over the loss of a patient whom the angel has just ushered into heaven. He longs to comfort her and assure her of her patient's newfound joy, but she cannot see him. His desire for her grows until finally he decides to make himself visible to her. They meet in a hospital hallway where Seth tries again to comfort her. With angelic sensors not attuned to earthly sensations of pain or pressure, taste or touch, his efforts at empathy and connection are limited.

Seth's natural curiosity about the human experience is inflamed by his growing desire for Maggie. The tension of their separation is resolved when he literally takes the plunge to exchange his angelic nature for that of a human. The camera offers us an intimate look at the fallen angel's discovery of the pain and pleasure of physical sensations: the throbbing of cuts and bruises he suffers from his fall, the delicious sting of a hot shower, the grainy sweetness of a fresh-sliced pear, and the transport of sexual union, a delight far beyond what he could imagine.

But life (or God?) is cruel. The next day Maggie is dead, the victim of a highway accident. Seth's newfound world is rocked by more pain than he could ever imagine. His angel friend Cassiel asks him, "If you'd have known this was going to happen, would you have done it?"

Trembling, his voice intense with grief, Seth replies, "I would rather have one breath of her hair, one kiss of her mouth, one touch of her hand, than an eternity without it . . . One."

In the final scene Seth relishes the cold tingle of salt water and wet sand surging over his feet. He body surfs with abandon while down the beach the angels revel in the transport of the sunrise.

And somehow, it's all the same, pleasure for pleasure. Except, to be completely honest, how many would think the angels' sublime sunrise connection with God looks more desirable than the shivering delight of the sun and the surf, much less an evening of enchantment with Meg Ryan or Nicholas Cage? Which is the more appealing "holiday at the sea"?

Our failure of wonder for God and lack of imagination for his invitation to live a kingdom kind of life are writ large in the stacked deck of this movie. The joy of God's presence is painted so small, the pleasure outside his kingdom so very large.

How can God help us imagine the heights and depths and lavish largeness of his invitation to Life? The Living Treasure who wants to give himself as a gift offers us pictures:

"You prepare a table before me in the presence of my enemies," sings the shepherd.

"The kingdom of heaven is like a king who prepared a wedding banquet for his son," Jesus said.

"'Blessed are those who are invited to the wedding supper of the Lamb!'" the angel cries out at the end of days.

"Trust me," I think God whispers, "your future with me is better than the joy of a wedding night. I invented wedding nights to give you a glimpse of what awaits. Your joy will grow more intense every day of eternity because you will know me better and see my glory more clearly, but it will take an eternity because my heart and my glory are infinite. The challenge and delight of reigning with me will far surpass a holiday at the earthly sea. My invitation is to a banquet, 'a feast of rich food full of marrow, of aged wine well refined.' A table loaded with heaping piles of comfort and hope and the sweet savor of my presence, dripping with the fruit of love, joy, peace—all the riches at the heart of large living."

No matter if you are confined to a hospital bed or kicking back at the Hyatt.

I've tasted and seen that God himself is the feast of Life.

And the enemy's table is a banquet in the grave.

When our lives feel so small because of illness or poverty or no husband or a husband who's too absent or too controlling or too many kids or not enough kids or a dead-end job or a job that sucks everything we've got into its relentless vortex, we may think our escapes enlarge life. Our secret adventures beyond the fence give our imagination room to breathe. Our wounds hurt so badly we want the enemy's banquet even if it is an illusion. Like the traitor, Cypher, taking a bite of his virtual steak in *The Matrix*: "I know this steak doesn't exist . . . (but) ignorance is bliss."

When we escape real life to indulge in our dream machines—the ones we looked at in chapter 4 (too much TV, too many hours cruising the net, chatting in virtual back rooms, one page-turner after another, not just ideas and pictures of what we long for but fantasies where we write ourselves in as the lead character in the story)—we eventually face the question: *What difference does it make if the life I enjoy isn't real? What difference does it make if all this time I'm spending in Neverland is not invested in real Life? If the pain and limitation of reality overwhelm me, if I am enjoying the journey as an "accidental tourist," why should I care?*

We each must answer this question for ourselves, but here is some of the wisdom I have found on my journey. Frederica Matthewes-Green has said, "Reality is God's home address." This simple bolt of the obvious struck the murky pond of my self-justifications, and all the reasons why I had felt so ambivalent about my escapes floated to the top. The more I thought about this truth, the more I realized that to live with integrity is to live in the present tense of the universe God created, rather than resorting to an alternate universe starring me as the Tap-Dancing Cosmic Blonde.

In 2 Corinthians 4:2, Paul says that we speak truth "in the sight of God." Reality is living in God's presence. If we truly want to love and seek God, we find him in reality, even painful reality, not in fantasy and distraction. To indulge in fantasy and vicarious enjoyment of the life I long for over the reality God invites me to be a part of is to set myself up as the creator of my own universe and separate myself from his design and purpose.

What is most real is eternal life. "And this is eternal life," Jesus said in John 17:3, "that they know you the only true God, and Jesus Christ whom you have sent." The real action of Life is in God's Story, and the heart of his Story is in relationships—seeking and loving God and others. Moving past my own pain to engage in the real battle for hearts. Holding fast when the fighting is fierce.

As I look back over my small-world season, I think how the emptiness I felt came from being in a place, either in my head or on a screen, where I was not present to God or other people. I was living a life divided between God's creation and my own. When we live in reality, we can breathe a prayer at any moment: *Lord, give me strength for the task, wisdom for the moment.* I can never think of a time when I was watching long stretches of TV or spinning my all-about-me tales when

I prayed a "help me" or even a "thank you" prayer. Quite the opposite. In the midst of my indulgences, I never thought about being in God's presence.

I sensed the lack of integrity deep in my bones. The reality of my own life, full of potential moments of love and service, was ticking by, and I was going to Disneyland! Or rather Fantasyland. Both in duty and escape, I was missing my moments. Wasting big chunks of my life. My escape was killing me softly—one evening of TV, one daydream at a time.

We hear Seth's declaration that "just one" moment with Maggie was worth far more than an eternity without her touch, even (he implies) if it meant an eternity without God. We shake our heads—an eternity without God? He can't even imagine. We know better.

But here is a question I ask myself: Am I making a similar choice about my moments every day? It's such a gray area. We need times of rest and recreation. But at some point, are we indulging in a life of escape and distraction when we could be savoring the present moments of real Life God offers us?

Before they hung Jesus on the cross, the soldiers offered him a little wine mixed with myrrh—a way to escape the full reality of his pain. Did you ever think seriously about why he refused? Living in reality, totally present to his Father and his suffering, meant more to Jesus than embracing a well-deserved escape. Like William Wallace in *Braveheart*, he had a battle to fight and wanted his wits about him.

God has issued his great invitation: *Seek me. Find me. Go out and find the people in pain and bind their hearts to me. Gather up the pieces of broken lives and release the captives; deliver my truth, my joy, my healing touch with the gifts and talents I have given you. Be my ministers of reconciliation. My Redemptor. My Redemptress. Take the risk. Move into lives. Infect others with your passion. I'll give you confidence and boldness. There is no ultimate risk because your name is written in the Book of Life. Rule and subdue, build and grow, and, yes, as the psalmist says, "Enjoy the good life in Jerusalem." But as you go, make disciples; watch for the kingdom doors I open along the way.*

My own experience was that when I diverted so much energy and imagination into an alternate universe, there was less left over for the real world. I would lose my creative impulse for daily living. "Leftovers again?" *Yes, and not just for dinner.*

The only way I grow and change and become the person God dreams for me to be is when I am present to reality, not lost in distractions and escape. I do not grow or change when my challenges are virtual. In fact, depending on my attitude, I think my indulgence can reinforce my worst self and keep me from growing. *I am so worthy. I deserve more than real life offers me!*

I've discovered that growing into the person God wants us to become takes every ounce of imagination we have. We have to dream of being a good friend, a lover, a Redemptor or Redemptress before we can do it. We have to pray about it and think about it, and then suddenly the ideas pop into our heads, or the doors swing open right before us. And because we've been trying to imagine what open doors might look like, we *recognize* them as opened doors and move on through. So many of us are spinning along in the orbits of our church and Christian friends that it takes a great deal of imagination to think how we're going to move out to build bridges to other people who need Christ.

There were times when I would hear God's invitation and think, *I love worldview. I have all this education. I read and keep files on how our families are squeezed into the mold of this world. I think about how to push back and live for Christ and his kingdom in today's culture. I ought to put some things together and offer a class or a Saturday seminar.*

But "life is just so . . . daily," as greeting card magnate Mary Engelbreit would say. Going with the family, work, and church flow, it would have taken a great deal of imagination to figure out how to take what I was learning and offer it to others in a helpful format. It always takes imagination to respond to God's invitations to ministry. I couldn't imagine how life could be more, given my limitations, and it never occurred to me to ask God to give me that vision.

I had creative moments teaching my college classes and playing with my son, planning birthday parties and musical programs for the church. But far too many of my creative impulses were zapped by the cathode rays emitted from my TV. So many good ideas and intentions melted into my blue Naugahyde recliner where I stared at the big hypnotic eye. "Trust in me, trust in me," it chanted, just like Ka, the cobra, in *Jungle Book,* with his mesmerizing gaze.

When, by his Spirit, God enabled me to close the door to my escapes, some of that creative energy finally found its way into teaching that class, organizing the seminar, writing a book. Once my creative momentum began rolling in the kingdom direction, more ideas began to flow. I saw more opened doors for the Life God offers. It's quite possible they were open before, but my imagination was too sidetracked to see the possibilities.

I don't want to give the impression that Life is mostly about *doing.* That once I started *doing* more intentional things for the kingdom, *that's* when I began to live the kingdom kind of Life. Reality truly is "God's home address." As I lived there in imaginative obedience, God drew near. The doing flowed from the knowing.

My publisher, Crossway Books, has given me a beautiful book of the Masonite drawings by Robert Doares picturing the life of Christ, *Immanuel, God with Us.* The original drawings hung in the Billy Graham Center Museum at Wheaton College, wide rectangles four feet across and fifteen inches high. Before and after Easter, I lay the book out on my sofa table, turning a page each day and letting the pictures take my imagination across two millennia, back to Jerusalem and Galilee.

In one of the final double-spread pictures, several paths converge on the top of a small mountain in Galilee. From the artist's helicopter view, a lofty cloudbank rises toward the northwest where the gospel would spread. A small robed figure thrusts one arm toward those distant lands, directing the gaze of eleven men seated in a half circle before him. The Scripture underneath the picture is Christ's commission to go out and invite others to follow him (Matt. 28:19-20).

As I walked by the table yesterday, I looked at that tiny group sitting in the curve of a path across a broad stony terrace in the sweeping landscape. The sheer measure of Jesus' invitation stopped me cold. Eleven men are invited to change . . . everything? All those miles and miles and city after city? How do you imagine a church? How you imagine missions? How do you take what Christ said and did and roll it out to a world that has never heard of Jesus of Nazareth, or the God of Abraham, or a church?

And then in the next breath Jesus left. He loved them and blessed them and promised he would be with them, and they were left with his invisible presence and power to figure it out—just as we are. The invitation and the potential seem overwhelmingly large. But they did it. They dreamed God's dream. They imagined God's kingdom—the extension of his rule in heart after heart, city after city, millennia after millennia. The joy, the challenge, the thrill of victory and the agony of temporary setbacks were theirs. We can trace the majesty of every cross on every steeple or altar, every Bach concert on a soaring pipe organ, all the missionary outposts and hospitals, every stadium packed with tens of thousands of people listening to Billy Graham or Luis Palau, even Larry the Veggie Tales cucumber—all of it leads straight back to that little half circle of men staring up into an empty sky and wondering, *What do we do now?*

To live large does not mean we can't live quietly and work with our hands. That too is a biblical ambition. God's invitation to play a significant role in his Story is offered to a quiet life as well as to a life with a little more noise. What matters is how we respond—how our vision and passion for God touches a circle of people and ripples through eternity.

To live small is to live hemmed in by the pain of our wounds and loss. To live in prideful rising and resignation, escape and entertainment. To miss the piece of mission that could be ours—the wonder of being a small part of something very big. We will never know what we could experience of God or his people or his adventure until we turn our hearts toward his invitation and put our distractions and escapes in their proper place—recreation. Re-creation and renewal to pursue the life we are offered.

How can we tell if we're living small? If our escapes and diversions are really costing us? If they are softly becoming the things we love and desire more than God?

I think of how Israel slipped into idolatry—a treaty here, an inter-marriage there. Once the Israelites settled into the land, it was much harder to push back from the table, turn off the TV, pack up their swords, and go out to battle against their idol-obsessed neighbors. Within a generation the idols captured their imaginations, crept into their inner worlds, and eventually invaded their national life.

"This is the way sin deceives," writes Edward Welch in his book *Addictions: A Banquet in the Grave.* "In order to slip past our consciences it must begin with small steps of disobedience."[28] Welch invites us to *name the thing we love more than God for what it is—an idol*—and describes falling into idolatry as a courtship, a progression from friendship to infatuation to love and betrayal and finally, worship.

My progression into that kind of courtship began from a heart divided between my dreams and God's dreams. A passion for the study and teaching of God's truth, but not the same delight for seeking the presence of God as a person. My involvement in church and a Christian lifestyle disguised both my lack of affection and the danger of my escapes. I didn't confess my lack of passion toward God because I couldn't imagine what I was missing. I didn't acknowledge my indulgences in escape and entertainment because I liked to think I wasn't over the line. *It's okay as long as it's all in my head.* When I began to have doubts and questions about my indulgence, I kept my thoughts to myself. I considered sharing them with my husband, but in all honesty, I didn't want to be accountable to someone that close to me. Besides, it was very embarrassing to talk about.

I needed someone to ask me, as Welch does in his book:

"Where are your affections?"

"What gets you excited? Depressed? Afraid? Angry? Hopeless?"

"What are these emotions saying about what you worship or what you love?"

Are you enjoying your times of personal worship of God?

"Are you confessing your own sin?"

How do you feel about going to church? When you don't feel like going, what nudges you out of your bed? The prospect of worshiping God or seeing your friends?

"Are you speaking honestly about your own spiritual lethargy?"

If you don't have a passion for God as strong as your passion for rising or escape, are you praying that God will change you?

"Are you alert to where your imaginations are reckless?"

Can others "speak openly to you, without fear of your anger, judgment, or sermons?"

"Do you invite others to tell you where you need to be growing? Where you are missing the mark in your relationships?"[29]

These questions invite us to step outside our busyness, shove past our Cosmic Blondeness, and, for Christ's sake, REFLECT. Take a long hard look at ourselves in the mirror of God's Word and do something about the pictures in our heads and the apathy in our eyes.

"Addictions don't just happen," Welch writes. "They need a mind that has set its imaginations and affections on its own desires." How does our imagination get hooked in? What does the progression look like?

Imagine we're sitting down together, perusing the pictures of a courtship—pictures from Welch's book that illustrate how the affection of a soul moves away from God and gets hooked into idolatry . . .

SNAPSHOT #1: FRIENDSHIP

Here we're "thinking about our idol more often." We clip articles and pore over magazines and join fan clubs. We run to check our e-mail and labor over our responses. We withdraw from our family and friends to spend time with it and with other people who share the same idol. Although we may think that time we devote to our idol is within proper balance—safely contained in the privacy of our head or our screens and within the bounds of our leisure time—the consequences begin leaking into other areas of our lives. We start spending considerable time and money, maybe even money we don't have, on our idol. Our indulgence is fun, and we feel totally in control, even more alive. We may feel nagging doubts about God's pleasure, but instead of laying it out before him, we prefer the "don't ask; don't tell" approach.

SNAPSHOT #2: INFATUATION

Here we are sneaking. Sneaking messages or chat. Sneaking around the Web looking for gossip or stories. Sneaking out to buy substances and hide them at home. We're covering up the way we think about our idol or the time we spend with it. Someone calls and asks what we've been doing. We may have been watching TV all evening, every evening, but we won't admit it. Our idol begins to affect our finances, marriage, or work. I can remember times of going out to do ministry without adequate preparation because I had spent too much time in my fantasies. Balaam's ass spoke with more integrity than I did. Rather than acknowledge our misplaced affections, we deal with the resulting tension by blaming our circumstances or other people. We devise occasions to indulge and avoid places where we can't. Promises easily made to lay our idol down, even promises made to God in confession, are quickly broken. We can stuff our idol in the trashcan before Communion and sneak it back out Sunday evening.

SNAPSHOT #3: LOVE AND BETRAYAL

Here we have our arms around our idol, and it is truly becoming an addiction—a near daily feature of our lives and treatment for every problem. We can create problems in the home as an excuse to resort to our idol. Lying becomes a way of life. Instead of learning how to deal with conflicts in relationships or work, we look to our idol to offer a temporary fix. We believe our idol is helping our self-image and giving us a deeper sense of worth and reality.

SNAPSHOT #4: WORSHIP

Our idol has its arms around us, not in an embrace, but in a death grip, separating us from God, our family, our friends, all the things that are truly Life. The idol becomes our master—the center of our life. We do not control it. It controls us. We're hurting many loved ones, but either we don't care, or our guilt drives us deeper into addiction and bondage to our idol. We still don't think we have a problem.

Blaming others, lying, increasing blindness to a rising that has become a falling into bondage—do you see any of these red flags waving in your life? I include these snapshots because I made a friendship with my idol and even flirted with infatuation without anyone sitting down with me and saying, "My friend, look at this progression. I worry about you because I see you taking steps down this path. Remember God's invitation to Life. To joy in reality, his home address. Seek counsel. Nothing is smaller than life on a short chain of addiction to anything we love more than God." If you have no one who will talk with you like this, then let me be that friend.

And one more thought about romantic fantasy in particular. Whether it's romantic fantasy, which we may tend to excuse, or pornography, which we know is over the line, when our imagination casts someone other than God or our spouse to meet our needs for intimacy and fulfillment, whether it's a photograph, a celebrity, a character from a story, or a flesh-and-blood possibility, it's like a slow leak that drains the desire from our relationship with God and our marriage. We can put the kind of creative energy into the fantasy that doesn't leave much for God or our spouse. Friendship and infatuation with romantic fantasy saps the vitality from our prayers and our passion for God. In our hearts we are no longer the one-woman man or one-man woman that God wants to lead his people.

A new reality is only one small step away from our imaginations. If we ignore the blinking lights and the striped gates, when we finally see the train coming, we can find we have no brakes. Afterwards, as we numbly survey the wreckage of divorce, we can often trace the skid marks of indulgence in romantic or pornographic fantasy right into the bloody severing of the husband-head from the wife-body. Betrayal is a nuclear bomb. Divorce is the end of a small civilization over which our children weep. God's mercy is new every morning, and his invitation is to live large. See where this progression is headed.

Please, my friend, by the power of the Spirit, turn your imagination to God and his Story of Life. Ask him to heal your heart and give you a new vision of the Life and reality he is calling you to be a part of. We will focus our imaginations on something. We can't merely turn off the wrong pictures. We need new ones to take their place. We'll talk more about this in the chapters ahead.

Do you know where your escape will lead? If it's like mine, it will quite simply lead to more escape. We may smile and shrug at clichés such as "familiarity breeds contempt" and "the law of diminishing returns," but they point to a reality that is relentlessly true. If we continue to choose escape, it takes more time, money, and creative energy to find the hatch. Our stay-at-home escapes grow into venturing-out escapes. While our desires and risks grow, our heart shrinks.

If God hadn't rescued me, if God doesn't rescue you, you may one day find yourself in a family wreck or in the place Douglas Coupland described in *Life After God*: "I've been losing my ability to feel things with the same intensity—the way I felt when I was younger. It's scary—to feel your emotions floating away and just not caring. . . . Loneliness had of late become an emotion I had stopped feeling so intensely. I had learned loneliness's extremes and . . . [realized it] was no longer new or frightening—just another aspect of life that, once identified, seemed to disappear. But I realized a capacity for not feeling lonely carried a very real price, which was the threat of feeling nothing at all."[30]

Alone at night we catch glimpses of where all this is taking us. Living close to God, we absorb the weight of his character—his truth and holiness, mercy and grace. We are like the tree in Psalm 1:3—solid, substantial. Unanchored to God's love and truth, cut loose from the ballast of his character in our souls, we float, rising to a life "all about me"—my endless amusement, my needs, my worries, my pain. Like the chaff in Psalm 1:4—vanity, smoke, empty, shallow. Always grabbing the gifts instead of thanking the Giver. A few self-help books, a quick and superficial confession, a promise to do better, and we can push that guilt feeling back into a far corner of our hearts and keep floating.

Over time, though, something happens to our souls: We lose the ability to feel the old highs of virtue and right living and victory in the struggle or the weight of guilt and failure and defeat. We can't sustain the lasting joys of love and intimacy or sense as deep a pain over loss. We can no longer empathize, and it becomes harder to even sympathize with others who feel that way. Os Guinness has said, "Sin is like spiritual leprosy. We can shred our soul to pieces and never feel a thing."

A heart created tender to God, with all the connect points and capacity to grow into the largeness of his heart, becomes scarred and shriveled, unable to feel. This is another high cost of living small.

God wants so much more for us. James tells us that "every good gift" is given by the "Father of heavenly lights." When Seth, the fallen angel, says he'd rather spend eternity with memories of the gifts than with the reality of the Giver, he denies the true longings of his own heart. He bends reality to fit his illusions. It is easier in the short run. But the longer he pursues the banquet in the grave, the more the losses of an eternity without God loom.

What is the ultimate price for living small? Our pictures of hell vacillate between stereotypical clichés of fire and brimstone that we don't really process and pictures of screaming and burning so hideous we don't want to look. We also don't want to wrestle with the questions: "How could a merciful God . . . ?" Perhaps it won't be the lake of fire for everyone who rejects God and his gifts. Scripture paints other pictures—"outer darkness." Hell is that picture of separation Jesus endured on the cross.

If God is light, if his good gifts include suns, stars, moons, aurora borealis, meteors, coal, petroleum and gas deposits, candle wax and nuclear fusion, then separation is black-hole darkness. Nothing to look at. No form or color.

If God has created everything we taste, smell, hear, and touch—food and flowers, music and silk—then separation means nothing delicious to eat. Stopped for eternity with no roses to smell. No wind or birds or sweet conversation to listen to. All those aging rockers who imagine hell to be a giant rock fest will have no guitars to play, no beer to drink.

If God has prepared a City with a splendor beyond words, then to lose heaven is not to join Satan in a kingdom hall or a throne, but in a lake. Imagine a lake with no scenery, formless and void, where fire and darkness hover above the face of the waters.

God invites us to a future of adventure and "reigning with him." Satan's invitation leads to an eternity with all the good gifts of opportunity withdrawn—nothing to do. All the gifts and talents God gave that were wasted on one's own pleasures will continue to be wasted but will yield no pleasure. Imagine a doctor with no medicines or hospitals, a teacher with no schools, an artist with no canvases, a chef with no kitchens or food. Imagine being discarded for eternity on the mother of all trash piles.

If God is the source of love and community, what happens to relationships when he withdraws his love and the power to deny our desires and give to others? In *Screwtape Letters* C. S. Lewis pictures hell as a bureaucracy—a feigned community where everyone glows with the pretense of wanting a relationship, but only as a front so their real intentions to betray and devour others will go undetected. Kind of like some working relationships in Hollywood. Or high school cheerleader tryouts.

But what if it's no community at all? If "it's all about me," then in the end what if it really is *that* and absolutely nothing more? No plot. No setting. No other characters to interest or even use. Just me. Alone in outer darkness. Living small beyond imagining.

If we don't want God on his terms, if we refuse him, and he withdraws all his good gifts—his creation, his invitation to grow and build and seek and find, his presence and his people, his hope, his future— what will be left?

The vacancy of hell. The grave with no banquet.

When I've tried to manipulate my reality with escape and imagination or substitute the false reality of endless entertainment and busyness for the kingdom reality that is God's home address, even though I am forgiven and reconciled to God, I've discovered that my life moves in the same direction of emptiness and loss.

We can think that if we have put our faith in Jesus Christ, our future with God will be all gain and no loss. But in 1 Corinthians 3:15 Paul reminds us that if we have invested this life in things of little value, we will "suffer loss." The tears Jesus "wipes away" may flow from the pain of realizing that so much of what we could have enjoyed for eternity is gone.

What we long for is the largeness of Life. And the Lord is our Life. I don't believe any of us turn to entertainment, daydreams, and virtual pastimes as the thing we really want. They are the Big Bird Band-aids we stick on our gaping wounds. The Twinkies we grab to give us a quick fix for our God-given longings for real Life in his Story.

Living in God's reality also leads to loss—loss of control and submitting to the truth outside us. As Os Guinness writes in *Long Journey Home*, "We have to face up to reality rather than trying to fit reality into our schemes [*and escapes*]. But the long-term outcome is freedom, because truth *is* freedom as we engage with reality as it truly is."[31]

God invites us to seek him at his home address and to live as large as we can in the real world of his kingdom. Will we "*perhaps* reach out for him and find him"—and find our dreams beyond imagining?

12

DRUMROLL

Picture me with my ground teeth stalking joy—
fully armed too, as it's a highly dangerous quest.
FLANNERY O'CONNOR

John's mind raced. Mary's words, tumbling and breathless, had shattered the pictures of pain that enveloped him. "An empty tomb . . . no guards in sight . . ." Peter's footsteps fell farther behind, but he couldn't process the sound enough to hold up or slow down. With his hand, then his sleeve, he wiped his running nose and swollen eyes. His mind grasped at dangling threads of past conversations somehow connected to Mary's words and traced them into tangles of things to come. He picked at the tangles but couldn't unravel them. Around him the world moved in slow motion, stretching and stirring coals to life, startled by the speed and intensity of the figure that sprinted past.

From the hedge at the garden gate a rustle of wings took to flight. The path dipped down through the rows of grapevines, past the winepress. Around a final corner, the tomb, bathed in rosy light, matched Mary's picture exactly. No stone. No guards. John slowed, scanning the shadows for swords and helmets. At the dark rectangular opening he paused and, bracing his hands on both sides of the doorway, leaned into the tomb, bending over, straining his eyes.

Where the body should have been lay only strips of unspooled linen. Some white. Others smeared and clotted with dried blood. The damp, moldy cold absorbed the heat radiating from his skin and the steam of his rasping breath. Gradually his breathing quieted. If he closed his eyes, the chaos of questions and images of slow death scraped his heart raw. If he opened them, the solid fact of the scene before him ignited a flicker of hope, a little flame that burned within the ache. He pulled back and slumped against the doorway.

Stumbling slightly and gasping, Peter shouldered past him into the tomb. Peter paused at the empty bier, surveying the pile of linen. Farther into the darkness he halted again, seemingly riveted by something John could not see. John stepped in and drew beside Peter. The burial cloth that had been around Jesus' head lay folded up on a ledge by itself, separate from the linen.

Peter turned to him, his eyes liquid with wonder, and left.

John saw and believed.

Creation, Fall, *redemption!*
Characters, plot, setting.
Lights, camera, action.
Seek me. Find me.
The Story unfolding around us is a Story of redemption. God takes what is broken and shines his glory through the cracks so we will "seek him and *perhaps* reach out for him and find him, though he is not far from each one of us" (Acts 17:27 NIV).

Perhaps, ah, there's the tension, the conflict . . .

Perhaps we will reach out . . .

Perhaps we won't . . .

We live in the drumroll of suspense.

Will we reach out for him, not just at the cross but today? And tomorrow? Can we imagine his presence through our day, the reality that shimmers through the dark glass?

In the final chapters of John's Gospel, the suspense builds as we wait to see if John, Peter, and the others will reach out and find Jesus. Mourning and weeping, bolted behind locked doors, the disciples cannot believe Mary's report. But John and Peter realize what is at stake:

If Jesus was alive, it would change . . . everything. They risk it. They didn't sneak through the shadows. They raced to the empty tomb. Neither could understand how all the pieces fit together. But John saw with the eyes of his heart and *believed* (John 20:8). He could imagine that God had raised Jesus from the dead.

The others struggled. All day reports drifted in. From the women. From Peter and John. Later that evening from the two disciples fresh from Emmaus. While they were telling their story, suddenly Jesus showed up in person, right through the locked doors. The disciples were startled and frightened. They thought Jesus was a ghost. He pointed to his scarred hands and feet. Their fright gave way to amazement. But the Son of God had to eat a fish before they finally "saw and believed." And the certainty of what they saw with their eyes and touched with their hands carried most of them through the drumroll of their own martyrdom.

The boredom of resignation and escape is impossible if we live in the everyday drama and suspense of the Kingdom Story. If we truly imagine what is at stake.

Our college-age son meets us for dinner. We laugh and talk and share stories. The plates are cleared, the bill is paid, the conversation winds down. He looks away and clears his throat. "Well, there's something I need to talk to you about." This is the moment I want to hear the drumroll and see ourselves in the middle of the Kingdom Story, so that as he shares his heart and seeks our help, I don't jump him. I don't dump my wounded feelings on him. If I hear the drumroll, I can listen and pray. *Okay, Lord, I can tell this is going to be hard. It's the battle. Help us. I'm reaching out. Please show up. In our tenderness. In whatever decisions we need to make.*

Realizing what is at stake for me requires a clarity of imagination. I need to see the enemy at work. I need to see a battle shaping up. Like David in the Psalms, I need to see life through the lens of war.

In his book *War Is a Force That Gives Life Meaning*, cynical war correspondent Chris Hedges finds moral categories of good and evil hard to nail down. He tries to persuade his readers that war is fought because of "myths" people believe. To those who "swallow the myth" that their cause is righteous and the enemy is evil and vicious, "life is transformed. The collective glorification [of war] permits people to abandon their usual preoccupation with the petty concerns of daily life. They can abandon even self-preservation in the desire to see themselves as players in a momentous historical drama. This vision is accepted even in the face of self-annihilation. Life in wartime becomes theatre. All are actors."[32]

"The world, as we see it in wartime, becomes high drama. It is romanticized. A moral purpose is infused into the trivial and commonplace. And we, who yesterday felt maligned, alienated, and ignored, are part of a nation of self-appointed agents of the divine will."[33] You can hear Hedges's sarcastic edge as he pictures the deluded people who believe the myth. But as a man who has seen more than his share of body parts, terrified children, and hidden mass graves, he makes some deeply true observations. When people see life through the lens of war, it changes everything.

When you are asked to think about life as war, how do you respond? Life is war? Yes, I believe that.

No, I didn't always. We live what we truly believe. I truly believed life was a stage, not a battlefield. If you go tap dancing across a battlefield, you're likely to get your Cosmic Blonde head blown off (which, now that I think about it, explains a few things). If I and if you truly believe life is war, then, just as Hedges tells it, we will abandon our "usual preoccupation with the petty concerns of daily life." We will "abandon even self-preservation" in the desire to see ourselves as "players in a momentous historical drama." That is what people do in real wartime.

Today is June 6, and TV and newspapers are filled with commemorations of the sixtieth anniversary of the D-day invasion of Normandy in World War II. In order to land 130,000 troops on a shoreline without harbors (where they wouldn't be expected), an entire nation had to drop their "petty concerns" and become "players" in winning the historic battle. In the segregated South, a small landing craft factory employing eighty people hired tens of thousands of whites and blacks, men and women, all working shoulder to shoulder, making the same wage. Troops trained, jumping out of cardboard boat-sized boxes and high-stepping through imaginary surf with their rifles up until they were exhausted. On the morning of the invasion, more than 2,500 Americans were shot, blown up, or drowned. Back home in New York's Grand Central Station, when the invasion was announced, a woman sitting on a bench sank to her knees in prayer, and then another and another, until almost the entire crowd kneeled to pray for God's mercy on their sons and countrymen. In wartime Grand Central Station became a house of prayer.

Some of us are war cynics like Hedges—spiritual warfare cynics. Not because we've seen too much of war like Hedges has, but maybe because we haven't seen enough of it. We look at the "romantic," war-like intensity of some of our brothers and sisters in the kingdom and wonder if they are overacting.

Should we truly imagine life as war? Can we believe it? What if we are not "self-appointed agents of the divine will" but God-chosen agents appointed to fight for our hearts and the hearts of others? What if we are called to abandon our "usual preoccupation with the petty concerns of daily life"? Take great risks? What if God wants to infuse his purpose into the "trivial and commonplace"—our errand list and our phone conversations? Is that being "romantic" or real? We can live our Cosmic Blonde days, as John Eldredge describes it, "as if we have landed on the beaches of Normandy in the early hours of D-day, June 6, 1944, with a lawn chair and a book to read. We are that unprepared for our lives."

I know my own penchant for performance and drama, and I've wondered if perhaps my growing desire to embrace life as war is another twist on the performance thing. I find my answer in Jesus' words and life. He described his purpose in terms of conflict over high stakes marked by intensity and great risk—the very essence of war.

I have come . . .

"to testify to the truth. Everyone on the side of truth listens to me." (John 18:37 NIV)

to bring conflict! Fire upon the earth! Not peace, but a sword, turning family members against one another. (Matt. 10:34)

"to destroy the devil's work." (1 John 3:8 NIV)

to bring Life! Life to the full. (John 10:10)

"to preach good news to the poor." (Isa. 61:1 NIV)

to proclaim freedom for prisoners and sight for the blind. (Luke 4:18)

"to release the oppressed." (Luke 4:18 NIV)

"to seek and to save what was lost." (Luke 19:10 NIV)

Jesus came to take sides and light fires, to fight for the hearts and lives of people who need him. To show us, in the bright fires of conflict, what a breathtaking treasure he is. It is *realism* that is prepared to endure extreme pain, loss, and no visible results—whatever it takes—to invite everyone into the fulfillment of all our deepest *romantic* dreams.

If Life is truly a larger Story of kingdoms in conflict, then truly *War Is a Force That Gives Life Meaning*. Not the "myth" of war, but real spiritual war with real casualties and victories.

We can pour our passion into chasing our visions of the small story we want to write, but what happens when we find our dreams, land a career? Then what? We find the love of our life, buy a home, and start a family. Then what? Whether we settle for less or chase small good-life dreams, life becomes boring because so little is at stake. *No tension or struggle to pursue higher hopes or dreams: no story = boredom.* Real Life with vision, passion, and intensity flows from seeing how Jesus lived and imagining what is at stake. Jesus does not offer me an invitation to include him in my nice Christian life. He offers an invitation to live in his larger Kingdom Story of conflict. Satan has engaged God in a battle for our hearts, and *the stakes of the choices we make in our everyday lives are far greater than I imagined.*

What is at stake?

People's lives.

I once heard Stephen Weinberg, a Nobel prize-winning physicist at the University of Texas, talking about his neighbors. "I have many friends who profess to be Christians. And I know what they believe. I know their creed tells them that if a person doesn't believe, that they will spend eternity in hell. But none of these people have ever talked to me about their faith.

"So I've come to the conclusion that either they don't take their own faith that seriously, or they're perfectly content to see me go to hell."

In defense of Stephen Weinberg's friends, they may have been completely intimidated to chat over the fence with a Nobel physicist about the ultimate reality of the universe. But the professor's comment raises the question: "Do we see life as war where the eternal life and joy of others are at stake?"

I have had to confess a lack of imagination about hell. Perhaps the reality was just so far beyond my experience or imagination that my heart couldn't connect. Or perhaps, growing up with an image absorbed in childhood, I never processed it deeply as an adult, and it remained something of an empty cliché.

Most of what we know of hell comes from Jesus' lips. Can we imagine what it would be like to endure even five minutes there of the suffering described in God's Word? Feel the nothingness of outer darkness? Hear the voices weeping and grinding their teeth and the roar of a burning lake? *Existence without God is so much more pain than I imagined.*

I grew up in a conservative evangelical culture that valued justice more than mercy. I am ashamed to admit that I tended to think that if people rejected Jesus' offer of forgiveness, well, they had made their choice. They deserved what they got. When I would share Christ, I sometimes left thinking, *Well, I've done my duty. The rest is up to them.*

It was a head reaction, not a heart reaction.

Perhaps the reason I've seemed "content" to let others face the ultimate reality of hell is because I also lack imagination about Jesus' love for people. I've not cared enough to fight for them or even walk next door and get to know them. Or, driven by my Christian duty, I've pursued a relationship to the point where I share my faith. I even invite someone to an event at my church. But if there still hasn't been any movement toward faith, although I don't mean to drop the relationship, it has sometimes faded.

I've come to acknowledge that this lack of love is connected to my dreams of rising, my preoccupation with my own dreams and fears. Christ tells me that if I am forgiven much, I will love much. If I think I'm living a nice Christian life, but I am not really ravished by God's goodness and holiness and realize how desperately I need his forgiveness, then I will not think I need to be forgiven much. And I will not love much. If I see myself as a fellow traveler with lost people, then my compassion grows. I realize that it's not that *they get what they deserve,* but *they suffer what I deserve.*

I wonder what would have happened if, in the parable of the prodigal son, the elder brother would have encountered his brother on the way home before the father saw him and ran to meet him. I can see him, hands on his hips, giving his brother the look—the slow gaze from head to toe and back up, taking in the ragged robe and torn sandals, a smile twitching at his lips. *Well, you got what you deserve.*

His heart seems so far from his father's heart. The father knows that the younger son deserves to suffer the consequences of rejecting the family. And, poor guy, there will be consequences. His older brother will inherit everything the father has while the prodigal will have to work for wages the rest of his life. Live as a guest, a hanger-on in his brother's house, or find his own meager lodgings.

But the father, the *father* longs to press that filthy kid's face to his heart.

There is not one shred of, *Well, he's getting what he deserves.*

The father's fight for his son's heart takes my breath away. He realizes what is at stake and risks holding his heart open to rejection. Granting his son's selfish requests. Writing off half the family wealth. Absorbing the pain of watching his son disappear over the horizon. While the older son withdraws from even the hope of relationship with "that son of yours," the father's heart stays open, vulnerable, watching, waiting, risking another day of empty horizon, another empty place at the table.

What am I prepared to do?

It has become incredibly painful for me to think of anyone spending eternity in hell. I rest in what Peter tells us Jesus did: He "entrusted himself to him who judges justly." And as Abraham affirmed, "Will not the Judge of all the earth do right?" *But while I trust, Lord, please help me to remember what is at stake and fight well.*

What is at stake?

Our joy.

When I think about other people's lives being at stake, I find myself slipping back into duty again. The guilt alarms go off; and I feel pushed rather than invited. If anyone should feel pushed into ministry, surely Paul could make the case. A light from heaven foiled his plans, blinded his eyes, and Jesus commanded him to go into Damascus where God appointed him to be "a herald and an apostle." But seeing people's lives change thrilled Paul to the core. The changed lives were his "hope, joy and crown."

God has given us a great gift—a ministry of reconciliation—an invitation to bind people's hearts to him and be a light to the nations, to let the prism of our lives refract the Technicolor beauty of God's glory. *The Message* paraphrases Jesus' words from his most important sermon:

> *Let me tell you why you are here. . . . You're here to be light, bringing out the God-colors in the world. God is not a secret to be kept. We're going public with this, as public as a city on the hill. If I make you light-bearers, you don't think I'm going to hide you under a bucket, do you? I'm putting you on a light stand. Now that I've put you there on a hill top, on a light stand—shine! Keep open house; be generous with your lives. By opening up to others, you'll prompt people to open up with God, this generous Father in heaven.* (Matt. 5:14-16 MSG).

Paul tells the Corinthians, "Such confidence as this is ours through Christ before God. . . . He has made us competent as ministers of a new covenant" (2 Cor. 3:4, 6 NIV). As we show others God's glory and love, he gives us competency: the creativity to imagine how to do it, the wisdom to carry out our ideas, the very words to say, and the prayers to pray to ask for his help.

We can pray strategically for the big "thy kingdom come" picture. *God, help me see what needs to happen for your will to be done on earth as it is in heaven.* From *The Message* paraphrase of Matthew 3:11-12, I have written this prayer in my journal: "Lord, may your Spirit ignite the Kingdom life within me like a fire. Help me see everything in its true and proper perspective before you."

I pray for specific, tactical "daily bread" ideas to accomplish the strategy: *Father, help me to imagine how to do what you want done. Especially how to love people.* Things or people come at us. It can be as mundane as the Latino laborer who wants to refresh himself from my garden hose or the church visitor seeking more than just directions to Sunday school. We can see them as intrusions in our lives or divine invitations to ministry. With a quick "Help me!" appeal for creativity, we can respond to any encounter as a ministry of reconciliation. God can also help us with endlessly resourceful ideas for taking the *initiative*. We hear the drumroll as we move into conversations, help a scared fellow traveler stranded by the side of the road, come alongside a friend whose husband is dying, and we hold our breath to see how God will move.

When we see God changing lives, our joy explodes. It is yet another way he shows us who he truly is. We are amazed and awed at how God gives us the grace to play a strategic role in his Story.

When I read the Psalms, especially David's prayers so full of enemies and battle, my concern is that I'll have no enemies because I'm not fully engaged in the war. I echo David's prayer, "*Lead me to the thick of the fight.*" It's unsafe and it's painful, but it's not boring. It's Life. And the second-rate pleasure of escape pales by comparison.

⚜

What is at stake?

Others' lives. *Our* lives.

Those of us who stand before the throne and the cross with assurance of forgiveness and heaven may tend to think the suspense is over. We've crossed the line of faith. We're in. "There is therefore now no condemnation" (Rom. 8:1). Growing up in my corner of evangelical Christianity, I saw the main thing as trusting Christ as Savior, getting to heaven, and then getting to work learning the Bible. Perhaps there is a link between that approach to faith and why I could love God as my foundation but still live in performance, duty, and escape.

I've come to wonder if we focused a larger portion of our message on crossing the line of faith and getting to heaven than Jesus did. Although Jesus talked about the kingdom so much—over 100 times in the Gospels—we rarely spoke of it, as if another corner of Christianity owned exclusive rights. When I read Jesus' words at face value, I can't help but notice that he doesn't merely invite us to enter or receive the kingdom. His invitation is to have a "kingdom kind of life" *now.*

God's kingdom, as Dallas Willard has so simply put it in *The Divine Conspiracy,* is where "what he wants done is done." If we are living the "kingdom kind of life," we will naturally "do what he wants done." "We will be so delighted in God, as people were with Jesus, that we will believe he is right." We will take him at his word and have faith that we will find more joy in what he promises than in what "sin promises."

When I was asked why I wanted to be baptized, I said something like, "Because I have trusted Christ as my Savior. I know I'm forgiven and going to heaven." It was the statement of a creed. And God loves creeds. Jesus came to testify to the truth. But if you were to ask me the same question today, I think I would respond, "Because I am captivated by God's beauty and love. I've fallen in love with Jesus, and I trust him for forgiveness and heaven and everything I need in between. I want to be the kind of person who will do whatever he wants done, including baptism." I still hold the creed, but I would want to make it personal—to pledge my love to my King and his kingdom. The difference between focusing on the creed rather than a shining vision of God and his kingdom sounds subtle but is part of what has moved me from duty to delight.

And I do so desperately want to be a "kingdom kind of person." In meetings, in discussions with Jack over finances, in conflict when my will is crossed, so often I don't even *think* about responding from the middle of the Kingdom Story, full of confidence and joy in God and his promises. Too often my first impulse is *^$@%*, and I have to constantly edit myself. Or ask forgiveness. My flesh seems set on a hair trigger, and the Spirit arrives on the scene when things are already in flames. But I'm thinking Story and suspense more often. And there are more moments of conflict when, by his grace, I do quite naturally exactly what God wants me to do with the vision and motives he wants me to have.

Willard writes, "It is God's intent that in his kingdom we should have as much power as we can bear for good." Really? It sounds too good to be true! And I'm back before the throne, astonished that he wants to ultimately share it with me because that's the kind of God he is. He is preparing me to reign with him. He wants to make us, as Willard writes, the kind of person he can set free in his universe and "empower us to do what we want. And when we are fully developed in the likeness of Jesus, fully have 'the mind of Christ,' that is what will happen—to his great joy and relief, no doubt."[34]

Whether I enter eternity as a two-talent or a half-talent, my sinful nature will be removed, and I'll see through the glass clearly. I'll share his joy—we all will. It seems we'll have an equal capacity to *choose* to do what God wants. But some of us may have the capacity to lead ten cities and others only a small neighborhood. Part of having a larger capacity to do what God wants is the ability to *imagine* how to proceed.

When our friend Vivian had arthroscopic knee surgery, Suellen and I spent the day caring for her. Now Suellen is a gold medal caregiver— mother of five, children's ministry director, sometimes caregiver to a mother struggling with dementia. Once we arrived home from the hospital, she quite naturally thought up all these ways to anticipate Vivian's needs. Which worked out fine because, while I offered a few things, I could sit on the couch and keep Vivian company while Suellen did many things I would have been glad to do if asked but couldn't imagine to offer. Things like, "Okay, Vivian, Scott will be home from the airport any minute. Here's your makeup bag. Can I run upstairs and get you some lotion or perfume so you'll smell good?" The experience of so many people to care for and years of seeking God's creative ways to care for them has given Suellen an imaginative and practical edge in caregiving.

Surely this is a picture of how our heavenly capacities will differ. I've grown up thinking, *Well, God will just wave the resurrection wand, and with no more sin nature, I'll naturally have all this capacity to reign with him.* But that's not the way he works now, and it's not how Jesus tells us it works in the parables of the talents and minas. Our capacity to imagine what Jesus wants done in our co-regency with him will flow out of a history of living close to him now, seeing how he does it, and having followed his creative lead. Our capacity to carry out what we imagine will come from the well of experience of kingdom problem-solving and risk with the talents he's given us here.

If I truly believed this, would I still whine or waffle about how to respond to the conflict in my life? If I could catch God's vision for the process, I might seek him and find him and more naturally do what he wants me to do.

What would happen if God took a Cosmic Blonde Tap Dancer and put her in a position of influence on a battleship? Would she operate more like the director on a cruise ship? Would she order pizza and movies for everyone? "Next stop, Utah Beach. Everybody be sure and get your goggles and fins." What if he appointed someone so task driven that while everyone swabbed the decks and polished the guns, the ship strayed off course and missed the battle? What if he appointed someone so fearful and insecure that she never came out of the officers' quarters except to inspect the lifeboats and run "abandon ship" drills? How can he entrust his future to us if we don't grow large enough to handle it? Where is the man or woman who can take that seat next to Christ on his throne and reign with imagination and experience?

The drum is rolling. What is at stake for us is not just heaven. It is the person we are becoming, and the outcome is far more critical than we realize. The kind of person I am becoming right now determines how much of God and Life I can enjoy now and my eternal capacity to serve and reign with the King. Fighting for such high stakes is risky.

As I have come to imagine the battle and the stakes and spend my creative energy on being strategic, the voices complaining about duty and resignation have given up and gone home. They couldn't compete with all the joy. If I'm "stalking joy," as Flannery O'Connor puts it, and taking risks to win the battle for my heart and the hearts of others, then I'll spend my big bucks on the larger Story instead of bizarre hobbies. If I live in the drumroll of real suspense, the invitations to escape into fantasy and virtual reality will offer all the appeal of a fancy plastic dessert that falls off the tray and bounces on the restaurant carpet. If I hold onto God through pain and loss, if I move against an enemy stronghold, I will know a sweet sorrow while I wait on God and a soaring joy when he does the impossible thing with impossible people.

Living by faith in the conflict and suspense with a clear vision of God's glory banishes boredom and the felt need to escape. With greater vision and imagination, God's grace sensitizes me to seize *kingdom opportunities* that would otherwise slip away in the routine of relationships and everyday living.

Opportunities to pray: When I see conflict shaping up, as in the restaurant conversation with our son at the beginning of the chapter, I can summon God's help to respond in the moment. If meetings are really worth attending, they will always be the scene of kingdom conflict, at least the challenge of creative tension. Going in with a heart prepared by prayer takes me out of my own agenda and into the larger Story.

I happen to live near a city that is an HVT, a high value target for terrorism. I also watch way too much news. Prayer takes me out of the Islamic terrorist war against the Christian/secular West story and back into the real Story where God is in control, and history is heading toward the holiday at the sea.

Opportunities to fight for the hearts of others: Without being obnoxiously "purpose driven" about it, I'm learning to look for opportunities to move past chit-chat, news, and ideas with questions about the life of our hearts. "How are you really thinking and feeling about life?" "How does this fit into the larger Story?" "This is how I've been struggling. What about you?" In response to conversations about a trial or a tragedy, I ask, "With all this going on, how is your heart?"

At a time when I was praying about pursuing a particular heart issue with my dad, he invited me to attend his sixtieth high school class reunion with him. The prospect of spending an evening with strangers twenty-five years older while my dad made the social rounds did not appeal to me. I declined. But when I remembered how I'd been praying, I called back with a yes. On the way home we had the opportunity to discuss what I had been praying about with great honesty and mutual concern. Plus I was the belle of the Geriatric Ball. When you are twenty-five years younger than every other woman in the room, you are youthful and gorgeous, and all the ancient football players hover around you like you are the long lost homecoming queen.

Opportunities to move out of my own circle of comfort so I can invite new people into the Story: I look for the visitors at church. I might opt to attend an art show opening by myself, rather than with friends, so I'll be free to connect. Or join a community group sharing my interests.

Opportunities to live strategically with my gifts: I think my place on the battle line is largely determined by my spiritual gifts of creative communication, seeing the big picture, and proclaiming truth boldly. I don't know if those are official gifts, but that is how God seems pleased to use me. I sift the demands on my time through the grid of my gifts and try to say yes where I can be used most strategically. And sometimes I'll "do windows'"because they need doing.

With gifts of communication there's always a trade-off between sowing broadly with many people, as with writing and speaking, and sowing deeply at the heart level with a few. I fight for the few. The few can always wait until later, which is why they need to be intentionally pursued. If I don't have time to call a hurting friend when I'm on a book deadline, then my book becomes another page in my small story.

This afternoon the evangelism team of our church met to plan strategy—a room full of talented people with a war-time budget. We told stories of sharing our faith. Some shared how they were reapportioning their giving to support the effort. Others told how they were withdrawing from other "good" ministry involvement to become more strategic in our own community outreach. Our intentional decisions encouraged one another. We dreamed. We prayed. We thought goals, strategy, and tactics. No one felt dutiful or resigned or bored. The air was electric, like the war room with the big map in the old movies where they push the armies and navies around with long sticks and the phones are ringing.

Living in the larger Story of God's kingdom rather than the small story of my comfortable Christian life changes everything far too much to mention here. And the longer I live in the larger Story, the more opportunities I see for change.

All the risk and suspense of becoming that "kingdom kind of person" and inviting others into the larger Story comes back to Godsight. I've had to see God and see what he wants in order to want to risk and engage in the battle. Godsight is the sheer, unmitigated joy of finding the hidden treasure of God in the unfolding Story of Life. It is an imagination ablaze with his present kingdom reality and his promises for a future far beyond all our good-life dreams. Godsight is Jesus Christ breaking into our distraction and duty and despair, just as he broke into the disciples' Easter evening wake, and turning hearts on a dime, infusing us with more purpose and plans and Life than we can ever imagine.

How does God grow a vision for him that fires our passion to be that kingdom kind of person?

Through suffering, choosing God, catching the vision of others who live and fight well, living with an awareness of life as a Kingdom Story of conflict and war, seeing God change hearts and lives—all the things we've talked about.

But the heart of the matter is, if we want to see God, we have to make the main thing the main thing.

THE MAIN
THING

All your wishes and hopes for the day rush at you like wild animals.
And the first job each morning consists in shoving them all back;
in listening to that other voice, taking that other point of view,
letting that other larger, stronger, quieter life come flowing in. . . .
C. S. LEWIS, MERE CHRISTIANITY

When *The Fellowship of the Ring* came to a theater near my friend Mollie, we grabbed two remaining seats on about row six and, with drinks in our cupholders and popcorn in our laps, settled back for the magical ride. The blazing big-screen battle swept us in—orcs, goblins, and ring wraiths hacking away at hobbits, elves, and dwarves, determined to recover the "one ring to rule them all" and deliver it to the Dark Lord who forged it.

Do you ever get so completely caught up in a movie's spell that you forget everything else around you? The flash and grip of the story rivets about 99 percent of your conscious attention so that only about 1 percent remains to direct the popcorn to your mouth and the straw to your lips. The people on your right and left disappear. The theater walls fall away.

Totally in thrall to this movie, at one point I reached for my drink, and the small, unengaged fraction of my brain recorded a dim, barely audible message: *Hmm, it's almost empty. How could this be? I don't remember drinking it . . .* After the last few sips I absently stuck the empty cup under my chair.

In the heat of the final battle, I reflexively reached for another sip of my drink, and that tiny part of my brain left behind in the real world noticed that now the cup was full. As I continued to sip long, deep draughts from a once-empty cup, the part of my brain still on real-world duty began summoning help to figure this thing out: *Why was my cup, once empty, now full? Had my cup really been empty?* The enchantment of the movie faded slightly. Eyes still on the screen, I leaned forward and, with my right hand, felt around under my chair and grasped . . . an empty cup.

My confusion reached a critical threshold sufficient to pry my eyes off the screen. I carefully inspected the *full* cup I held in my *left* hand, which I had taken out of the cupholder on my *left*. I distinctly remembered that Mollie had purchased bottled water, which I could see sitting in the cupholder to her left.

I looked back to the *right*, staring at the empty cupholder for several seconds, thinking about the empty cup under the right side of my seat. The Dr Pepper flavor in my mouth turned sticky and dry. Without moving my head to attract attention, out of the corner of my eyes I began a slow-motion scan along the arm and shoulder and up to the face of this rather bulky, side-burned fellow sitting beside me.

I can only say that the enchantment of the movie was completely broken.

For the remainder of the movie I fiercely debated whether, when the credits rolled, I would grab Mollie and run or, like a good Christian, acknowledge my sin and seek absolution.

After the movie I turned to the not-too-friendly face on my left and, with a weak laugh, said, "I am so sorry I drank your drink."

"Well, I kind of wondered . . ."

***

God has given us the gift of *intensity*—intense focus, interest, scrutiny, joy, sorrow, conviction, commitment, desire. And he has written a Story meant to rivet our hearts and minds far more than Tolkien's epic saga—a real-world adventure, deeper and higher than even our caffeine-enhanced capacity to engage can take in. The greatest commandment is about intensity: "Love God with *all* your heart, soul, mind and strength." Again and again throughout Scripture he invites us to . . .

. . . turn to him with all our hearts.

. . . trust him with all our hearts.

. . . serve him with all our hearts.

. . . obey him with all our hearts.

. . . in whatever we do, work at it with all our hearts, as working for the Lord.

What God wants is intensity. The intensity of war. Desire.

If there is one word people use to describe the movie *The Passion of the Christ,* it is *intense*—not just the beatings and nailings, but the way Christ keeps relentlessly giving himself. Offering his back to the whip. Dragging his body onto the cross. With an intensity excruciating to behold, he lays his life down. We can imagine that the actual scene was even harder to watch—those eyes fixed on the people who surrounded him, welling up with love.

If God pursues us with such intensity, if he poured his creative soul into designing a world and writing a Story—all "so that we will seek him and reach out for him," then we should not be surprised when he promises us that "you will seek me and find me. *When you seek me with all your heart*, I will be found by you" (Jer. 29:13-14, emphasis mine).

We are invited to *seek* God with an intensity that honors his desire for us. "Seek me," God calls to us.

"Seek me with all your heart and all your soul."

"Seek me urgently, while I may be found."

"Seek me first; I'll take care of all the rest."

"Seek me always."

"Seek me earnestly. I'll reward you."

"I will test you to see if you are really seeking me with all your heart."

This does not look like holding our Bible in our laps and reading it at commercials. It looks like sharing our food with the hungry, being available to our own flesh and blood, turning from sin with fasting, mourning, and praying.

It looks like David, who wrote:

> . . . *earnestly I seek you; my soul thirsts for you, my body longs for you . . .* (Ps. 63:1 NIV)

> *One thing I ask of the LORD, this is what I seek: that I may dwell in the house of the LORD all the days of my life, to gaze upon the beauty of the LORD and to seek him in his temple.* (Ps. 27:4 NIV)

> *My heart says of you, "Seek his face!" Your face, LORD, I will seek.* (Ps. 27: 8 NIV)

Surely this is seeking at its most basic: *"Seek my face."*

To seek another person's face means to seek his eyes: "Notice me!" Seek his ears: "Listen to me!" And seek his words: "Talk to me!"—the things we feel and say when we've been home with small children for a week straight and our spouse walks in. These cries for connection echo through the pages and the ages of the Psalms, pleas of intense longing for the presence of God. This is the main thing out of which all our other seeking flows.

As I look back on years and years of "quiet times," I see a girl, a young woman, and a maturing woman who spent hours beyond counting reading my Bible and praying. But I wonder how much of it was "seek your face with all my heart" seeking? I have learned about this kind of seeking from King Josiah.

Josiah became king of Judah at age eight. "In the eighth year of his reign, while he was still young [age sixteen], he began to seek the God of his father David" (2 Chron. 34:3 NIV). King David was his "father" in the sense that he was Josiah's ancestor. Josiah did not learn how to seek God from his own father. King Amon worshiped the idols of *his* father. Josiah never walked by the way while his father told him stories of what God was doing in his life. Amon never read to Josiah from God's Word. In fact, no one in the king's household or in all Israel could read from the sacred scrolls. The Book of the Law had been lost, and the temple, chock-full of idols and home to male shrine prostitutes, had fallen into disrepair.

Picture Josiah entering the dirty, dilapidated temple, passing the horses and chariots that the wicked kings of Judah had dedicated to the sun, and seeing the altars built by Manasseh where Josiah's father had sacrificed to idols. And yet, "neither before nor after Josiah was there a king like him who turned to the LORD as he did—with all his heart and with all his soul and with all his strength" (2 Kings 23:25 NIV).

Josiah sought God regardless of what his father did or didn't do for him, regardless of whether he attended a "good church," even without "quiet times" of reading his Bible. Maybe he prayed with a God-seeking friend or family member. Perhaps he walked the palace rooftop and listened to the stars sermonize every night or heard God's crashing thunder-voice echo through the Jerusalem hills. He sought and found God apart from so many of the things we tend to use and even substitute for seeking him ourselves.

In *Long Journey Home*, Os Guinness recalls a conversation about the intensity of seeking, saving faith recounted by an African missionary. A Masai warrior in Kenya rejected the Europeans' translation of seeking faith. "Your word means only 'assent' or 'agree.' [That is like] a white hunter shooting an animal with his gun from a great distance. Only his eyes and fingers took part in the act.

"True belief is like the lion pursuing his prey. His nose and eyes and ears pick up the prey. His legs give him the speed to catch it. All the power in his body is involved in the terrible death leap. . . . And as the animal goes down, the lion envelops it in his arms, pulls it to himself and makes it part of himself. This is the way a lion kills. This is the way a man believes. This is what faith is."[35]

Four years after Josiah began to seek God, at age twenty, the intensity of his seeking spilled over into an intensity of action—open warfare against the not-so-secretly indulged and broadly tolerated idol worship of his kingdom. Many in Judah and Jerusalem were worshiping God in the high places built to sacrifice to idols, instead of in the temple in honor of God's commands. Josiah lit out on a holy rampage against this half-hearted seeking, desecrating the high places with human bones, smashing Asherah poles, cutting the idols to pieces and sprinkling them over the graves of those who had sacrificed to them, maybe even his own father's grave.

How does that kind of intensity strike you? A little too hot? Do we want the intensity that God loves? Perhaps like me, your life has been a journey of halting, periodic steps to seek him amidst the great distractions in our lives. We slip into a casual, comfortable Christian life. We admire the Josiahs from a distance because up close they make us feel like the sluggard in Proverbs who has fallen into his recliner and can't get up. Every day the invitation comes to us afresh: *Seek me. Seek my face with all your heart.*

Seeking the Lord's *face* means . . .

Our eyes riveted on him, undistracted.

Our lips to his ears.

Our ears to his lips.

Something so simple it can be done from a hospital bed in extreme weakness.

Something so difficult that few of us do it well.

You will seek me and find me when you seek me with all your heart.

Somehow seeing and finding God is linked to our wanting him.

The question is, *How much do we want him?*

⁂

To be honest, *wanting* to seek God's face has been my greatest struggle. As with the issue of obedience, it means moving from duty to desire. Disengaging from the "wild animals" rushing at me to turn my imagination and heart to him seemed like such a *discipline*. Like going to the gym and eating rabbit food and working on your taxes and that whole list of things that carry an instant Rorschach association to totalitarian oppression and guilt.

I would begin the day thinking, *Well, I can get up early to be with God or sleep.* Once I was up and going, my activity-loving soul would often look over the day and say, "I can break away to be with God or get to work." In my leisure moments I could seek his face or do something fun or relaxing—*talk on the phone, read a book, go shopping.* Face time with God seemed so far removed from the action, so still and quiet when I was humming. It was hard to idle the engine that long. A short dip a few times a week was about as intense as I wanted. I've had to ask myself, *Is that consistent with how I seek other people or things with "all my heart" intensity?*

Although I loved God and felt he welcomed me, maybe *because* I understood I could come boldly before his throne of grace, I think I confused the easy access with the reality of entering his presence.

What did it look like when I took time to seek his face?

In community on Sundays, after a flurry of ironing, finding Zach's shoes, buttering toast, and keeping one ear attuned to the scorekeeping chat of the morning news shows, I often arrived on the church doorstep without one thought of anticipation for God or a heart in any way prepared to be with him. I visited with friends and family until the music started, at which point I sang the songs thinking as much about the notes as the words, processing the lyrics much the same way I did the sermon. Listening to the message with the same mind-set as my seminars on the History of Ideas—taking in information, truth about God. Enjoying truth. Delighting in the facts of who God is and the stories of what he has done, but rarely seeking him directly or responding to him as a person in his house, except for a few brief minutes in prayer or once a month during Communion.

Very little of my in-church conversation with friends centered around how we were seeking God or how he was being found by us. We shared prayer requests about the safe things—health, jobs, our children, other people, and calamities—things for which we were not responsible. King David may have been eager to speak in the assembly about confession and courage, warfare and wonder. But I think if he had dropped into our circle, we wouldn't have known what to do with him.

My times alone with God were often driven more by the enjoyment of study than the desire to seek his face. A summer without weekly study questions could become a summer of quiet times so quiet as to disappear. When I wasn't reading the Bible to answer study questions, I would read a chapter much the same way I read *Time* magazine—enjoying new insight, with little connection between my reading and my seeking. My prayers resembled the requests shared at church. Not much wonder or praise. Short on thanksgiving. Nice and long on the requests lists.

As with my experience of watching *Fellowship of the Ring,* I am capable of great intensity. Rapture over romance and music. Desperation over loss of relationship and missed opportunities. At some level perhaps I knew my intensity in seeking God paled beside my other intensities. But I never deeply considered whether "God is your unshakable foundation" was the same as seeking him with "all your heart" intensity. I am learning the difference.

If, in the midst of the winking and blinking of all our electronic screens, the allure of glossy pages of catalogs and magazines, even the billboards by the roadside, we are going to see the One who is invisible like Moses did, we must shut down the distractions and turn the eyes of our imagination to him.

"Lift up your eyes on high and see: who created these?" (Isa. 40:26). In his commentary on this verse, Oswald Chambers challenges us:

> The test of spiritual concentration is bringing the imagination into captivity. Is your imagination looking on the face of an idol? Is the idol yourself? Your work? Your conception of what a worker should be? Your experience of salvation and sanctification?

I would add, is it your dreams, your distractions, your vacation, your car? Is it even a ceaseless preoccupation with your spouse or your children?

> Then your imagination of God is starved, and when you are up against difficulties you have no power; you can only endure darkness. If your imagination is starved, do not look back to your own experience; it is God Whom you need. Go right out of yourself, away from the face of your idols, away from everything that has been starving your imagination. Rouse yourself, take the gibe that Isaiah gave the people, and deliberately turn your imagination to God.[36]

If seeing and finding God is linked to our wanting him, how does our imagination focus our desire? How can we direct our imagination and the *eyes* of our heart to *see* him?

We are wired so differently. Gary Thomas has written an insight-

ful book on all the different *Sacred Pathways* we take into God's presence. Some of us find our most direct connect to God's heart through
creation. Isaiah invites the people to *look to creation* and imagine the
One "who brings out the starry host one by one, and calls them each
by name." Too many of us are surrounded by too much concrete. Take
a walk. Really look at God's trees and night sky—all the signposts to
his beauty and splendor. Let your delight in your garden or the lake in
the park lift your eyes to his.

I love books. Bible study. Digging deeply into Scripture to discover
the author's intent. But I am learning to read the Word "slowly, *imagi-
natively*, prayerfully and obediently," as Eugene Peterson puts it.
"Imagination is the capacity we have of crossing boundaries of space
and time, with all our senses intact . . . finding ourselves at home in
Bible country."[37] Without a doubt, except for the thirty-three years that
Jesus walked this earth, *the way most of us see God most clearly is
through his Word.*

I find myself reading the Gospels over and over, picturing how the
expressions on the Pharisees' faces hardened as Jesus spoke to them. I
see him spring their traps and dissolve their saccharine, condescend-
ing smiles. I see him weep with longing over Jerusalem. And I see the
One who sits on the throne for eternity ride through its streets on a
donkey, like a late-night comic's parody of a conquering Caesar on
parade.

When I read the Bible's promises and prophecies and take time to
savor the celebration sure to come, the joy and beauty make me ache.
From the deepest pain and in the same breath that he makes his desperate requests, David often celebrates God's help long before the Lord
actually answers. In Psalm 56:2 he pours out his heart cry to God: "My
enemies trample on me all day long." In verse 13 he imagines, "You
have delivered my soul from death . . . that I may walk before God in
the light of life."

By fixing our imagination on God's fulfillment of his promises, we
can see his beauty in the darkness. In the wait. *God will come through.
The only question is timing.* When I despair over broken relationships
with other believers, when I cannot draw close because the other person wants to wound me or build a wall of distance, I picture us walk-

ing and laughing together in the future God has planned for us, enjoying for eternity the intimacy that seems out of reach for now. Prayers of imagining celebration ring with a confidence that grows even as we give them voice.

What a soul delight it is to see God in action in the Story of Life. To journal my praise and savor the moment between God and me. *God, you showed up! I called on you, and you kept your promise.* I have one journal that is all thanksgiving. As I write the stories down, it helps me to remember so I can share them with others. Karen Mains suggests specific strategies for seeking and finding God in everyday activities in her enchanting book *The God Hunt*. Together with her family they have learned to look for, record, and celebrate Godsight:

. . . answers to prayer,

. . . any unexpected evidence of God's care,

. . . any help to do his work,

. . . and any unusual linkage or timing of events, circumstances, or resources.

As I seek God's face, I look into the depths of his heart. I see a corresponding depth in my own heart. Proverbs says, "The purposes of a man's heart are deep waters" (20:5 NIV). And the psalmist adds, "Deep calls to deep." Jack laughs and counters, "Yes, and deep calls to shallow puddle." He's a little Blonde too. Yet, as I look on God's face, as I "pour out my soul" like David, "empty out the pockets of my life," and "open the heart of my book to his eyes," I learn to reflect and think critically about my own life. My Blonde soul deepens. Instead of skimming through the sunbeams, I see a pilgrim who stumbles repeatedly—wastes time here, gets lost there, says shockingly stupid things—and runs too hot, too cold. Loses faith. But when I see my reflection in his eyes, I see a woman in whom he takes great delight, like an artist who envisions the final picture and is delighted with his work in progress.

When our imagination falters, we can pray, "Lord, open my eyes to see you in all your Technicolor splendor." I wish I had begun praying this prayer a long time ago. If we lack vision, we have only to ask, and he will give it. "The LORD is near to all who call on him, to all who call on him in truth" (Ps. 145:18 NIV). Our vision will ignite our passion to seek him with ever more intensity.

If seeing and finding God is linked to our wanting him, how can we focus our imagination and direct our conversation to his *ears*?

Prayer and I have a long history. It is the one area of my life where I have diagnosed myself with ADD. The autobahn in my brain has no speed limit, and I have slick European sports car thoughts, which can be a good thing for creativity but a bad thing for prayer. Back in the old days, when all I wanted to do was drive through the back of the throne room and shout a brief, "Good morning. I'll be off now! Please bless me!" I didn't struggle so much.

My invitation to serious kingdom prayer came from a friend. Actually Jesus had been inviting me for a long time, but one year Diane took the podium of our weekly Bible study and was harder to ignore. "We are going to study prayer, and each week you will have assignments in *The Disciple's Life of Prayer.*" Outwardly I smiled, determined once again to tackle "the discipline of prayer." Inwardly . . .

In her cheerfully soft-spoken, inspiring way, Diane was the prayer Nazi who pushed past my wishy-washy Miss Scarlett "I'll think about that tomorrow" attitude and insisted, " You . . . vill . . . pray." My short irregular trips to the throne lengthened and focused. I fulfilled my weekly assignments, still more out of duty than delight. But the thing about a discipline is, the more you dig in against your old mind-set and habits, the more you become free to enjoy what used to look so daunting.

I've discovered that if I don't want to talk to God much, then I do not see him as he really is. Everyone wants to talk to his or her beloved. The more I love someone, the more I want to talk to him or her. And who among us would not accept an invitation to dine with a good, strong president of our nation? The entire pecking order in Washington is determined by how much access and face time you have with him. Our God is our beloved and the King of the Universe, and we can have unlimited face time. How can we not want to spend time and talk with him?

The more I see of God, the more I surprise myself by wanting to pray more.

I've also come to realize that if I can't do what I want to do—seeking God's face from delight rather than duty—prayer is perhaps the best thing I can do to move toward where I really want to go. If I find myself in more duty than desire, I can ask for desire. *Father, give me the intensity. Help me to love Jesus as much as you do.* And I'm praying Jesus' prayer for us in John 17:26: "Father . . . I have made you known to them . . . in order that *the love you have for me may be in them*" (emphasis mine).

I once read from some inspired source that I cannot now recall, "Prayer is at the heart of the action." It is the lifestyle of David, pouring himself out in prayer and plunging into battle. If we see life as conflict and risk, if we engage in the battle, then prayer will be as natural as breathing and the most important thing to be done. The days we don't, we'll feel the disconnect. Like driving around without a seatbelt.

I am so activity-oriented. I want to go *out* to the action scenes of life, not *in* to the quietness of my study. God has had to do more than slow me down with arthritis to get me alone with him. He's had to show me, as John Piper says, that prayer was never meant to be an intercom from our nice, comfortable house to the throne. It was meant to be a walkie-talkie from the midst of conflict to Command and Control. I have been learning to put on the armor and *pray*. As God has shown me his beauty in the suspense of the conflict, I am moving past the "discipline" barrier and discovering the treasure.

If seeing and finding God is linked to our wanting him, how can we focus our imagination and direct our ears to *listen* to his voice?

Josiah has taught me that seeking God's face is not exactly the same thing as Bible study. He sought the Lord for years before the book of the Law was found. Perhaps, in the oral tradition of his people, he meditated on the Psalms of his forefather David. But when the book of the Law was discovered and read to him, he listened. Overwhelmed at how his life and the lives of his people did not resemble the life of worship and obedience described there, Josiah tore his robes. He gathered his people to the temple, and, standing by the king's pillar, he personally read to them so they could listen to the words of God. He repaired the temple and re-instituted Levitical worship, providing Passover lambs to all the people at great personal cost so they could taste and see the joy of worship and seek God with all their hearts. When Josiah finally could read and respond to God's Word, he was able to seek God through worship and obedience in ways he had never known before. But Josiah began to seek God years before he enjoyed the privilege and blessing of reading Scripture.

We can read the Bible all our lives and miss the way Josiah sought and found God. We have a deep need for God to reveal his truth to our understanding *and* his real presence to our hearts. When we read God's words, intent on understanding, we find ourselves in the flow of a study mode, processing the truth and meaning of his words. We can miss his presence, though, if we do not listen to him as a person speaking directly to us and respond with a heart to obey.

God's presence in his Word shines more clearly as I've learned to read in small snippets and reflect. I try to imagine what that truth would look like in my life and give him a quiet pause to amplify or drive home what his words say. After we read a passage for meaning, we can go back and pray through what we've read, turning the verses into requests for ourselves, our family, our friends, church, country, and missions. It's much closer to a conversation where I speak and listen than reading for a time and then praying. And it's a conversation driven by things that are on God's heart, things I might never imagine to put on my list.

My cousin-in-law, Phyllis, was shopping with her size-two-and-a-half daughter, Autumn, a couple of years ago, whining about how she couldn't fit into any of the cute styles. Her daughter turned to her and said, "Well, Mom, if it really bothered you that much, you would do something about it." Phyllis shut her mouth, signed up to sweat at the health center, and just did it. Now she's the grandma every one wants to look like when they're a grandma.

If we want something intensely, we will go after it. We all read in God's Word what a treasure he is. We all hear how others grab hold of God in prayer and tell of finding the depths and the riches. We all know we have to learn the discipline of turning our imagination to God and seeking his face to find the delight. Prayer, praise, worship, confession—this is our deepest heart's way of Godsight. And if we don't just DO IT, we can't imagine what we're missing.

The more I turn my imagination to put myself in God's presence, the more I want to seek his face. But the more I look at God and my life, the more I see how relentlessly he has been seeking me.

When Zach was five years old, my mother and I drove into downtown Houston for an extravaganza of laser lights, fog machines, and fireworks. The sleek, glassy skyscrapers served as stage and screen for a show billed as unlike anything ever seen before. Tens of thousands of cars jammed all the in-bound arteries until, when all the parking downtown was full, the traffic stopped. We were about to turn right into a three-lane in-bound thoroughfare. The light turned, but we didn't. Our street became a parking lot. We opened the car doors and took a minute to decide what to do. Looking at all the parked cars around us, we decided to leave the car, lock it where it stood, and search on foot for a good vantage point. When we turned around to tell Zach, "Let's go," the backseat was empty. We looked up and down our street and the street we wanted to turn on and saw nothing but rows and rows and miles and miles of parked cars. No Zach.

Frantically we approached car after car until we found someone who said she saw a little boy walking toward downtown between the rows of parked cars and vans full of child molesters and every danger I could so easily imagine in the darkening city streets. My mom took off running in the direction where Zach had disappeared. I continued to comb the area around our car just in case the helpful stranger was wrong.

About three hours later, although my watch only registered ten minutes, my mom returned with my boy. Sweaty and panting, she and I collapsed onto the hood of our car in a post-adrenal meltdown. She had found Zach skipping merrily back toward our car, ready to escort us to the good location he had scouted out. He thought he was seeking us, completely unaware of his danger and how intensely we were seeking him.

I am so often like Zach—the best intentions and a general isn't-life-good, casual kind of seeking, but oblivious to the danger and my real need. I blunder into my Father and think, *Oh, I've found you!* Only because He has been seeking me with an unrelenting intensity. The intensity that took him from the throne to the cross. An intensity so fierce and yet to my unseeing eyes and dim imagination, so easy to miss.

He is seeking me like he sought Josiah. The king's ungodly family, the desecrated temple, and no Scripture to read—none of those things mattered.

God seeks me through his messengers with sledgehammers. Through the friend who invites me to pray. Through a godly future husband who meets me at a singles' pool party. Through my mom who gives me a book that opens my eyes to the study of worldview. Through the verses that pop off the pages of my Bible—just *the* verse I need for *that* moment.

God seeks me in church through a worship leader who doesn't just lead the music but directs me into God's presence. Through a heart that doesn't always sing, but listens, letting the music wash over me. Through a husband who *compels* me to *respond* to his message from God's Word. Through another friend who casually mentions how he was playing his guitar and reading Psalms on his porch one Sunday morning, preparing his heart for worship, and has no idea how his words have inspired me.

God comes to us through closing doors of distraction and opening doors of ministry. Frederick Buechner writes in *The Hungering Dark* that Jesus "comes in such a way that we can always turn him down . . . comes to us in the hungry man we do not have to feed, comes to us in the lonely man we do not have to comfort, comes to us in all the desperate human need of people everywhere that we are always free to turn our backs upon."[38]

We have no idea, really, how intensely our God seeks us. The same Masai warrior who saw faith as a lion's kill gives us a glimpse. "You told us," he said to the European, "of the High God, how we must search for him, even leave our land and our people to find him. But we have not done this. We have not left our land. We have not searched for him.

He has searched for us. He has searched us out and found us. All the time we think we are the lion. The lion is God."[39]

And I picture him, the Lion of Judah, Aslan, fully extended, leaping up the rocks, stalking us in the dark. I picture Jesus, arms open wide, not in desperation, but in intense longing: "Lael, Lael, how I have longed to gather you into my embrace. But too often you wouldn't let me. Not the way I wanted to."

So he bounds ahead and turns to face me, head lowered, tail twitching. Dangerous in his mercy. Threatening in his compassion.

14

INTO THE
FATHER'S ARMS

*Unless we get hurt right out of every deception about ourselves,
the word of God is not having its way with us . . . but the
point of the hurt is the great point of revelation.*
OSWALD CHAMBERS

Lauren sipped her coffee, scanning the headlines of the paper left, as always, in a mess on the table. *For once it would be nice if I walked into a clean kitchen like he does every morning.* A Democrat was going down in the flames of scandal he so richly deserved. She guessed. She didn't really know the details. But he was a Democrat.

The Sunday morning talking heads were all over it. While she put on her makeup, they were dishing up the details with a gleam in their eyes. She drank it in like a second cup of coffee. An extra kick for the day.

When it was time to leave, her keys were not by the back door. *Kara! Where are my keys!* Her daughter had left early with Andy for youth praise team practice—and . . . no keys. Lauren went upstairs and opened the door to Kara's room.

It was a good thing Kara was safely at church. Hot, molten wrath poured out of Lauren's soul at the chaos of clothes and papers and CDs and shoes and books and pizza boxes and makeup and cereal bowls before her. Surely this was not the fruit of her own orderly womb.

Kara, you are a pig no a pig is too dignified you are a rodent a bottom feeder how can you profess to love Jesus and wallow in the darkness of this valley of the shadow this Gehenna full of rotting garbage and look at those nice wool slacks with tomato paste you're going to have to pay to have them . . . And there were Lauren's keys on top of the wool pants.

Gingerly Lauren picked her way through the quagmire, fearful that underneath the lily pads of garbage and clothes there lurked a trash-feeding animal or Kara's guitar. She could see herself driving to church with a shoe on one foot and a guitar on the other. *Andy, help me. I had to walk through Kara's room.*

She left the always-closed door wide open. Her mark of territorial visitation and a sign to Kara. *I know. I know, and your sins have come up before me.* In the car she turned up the praise music loud enough to drown out the script that her old nature desperately wanted to rehearse.

Lord, the enemy is not going to ruin my Sunday. I love church. I love to worship. I love hearing the Word and seeing my friends. She belted the praise lyrics along with the CD, and by the time she arrived at church, all the heat was bottled and capped and stuck on a shelf in the refrigerator, and she would not open it until after lunch. But then . . . She smiled at Kara as she passed her on the back row and found the open seat beside Andy.

The sermon ran predictably late, which wouldn't have been so bad if Ron could just lighten up a bit. Tell some stories. Lauren really didn't care so much about the different views of prophecy. Jesus was coming back. Amen. Hallelujah. He could save Kara a lot of misery if he'd do it before they finished lunch.

Three pastors in nine years. And Ron isn't faring so well either. Soon Andy will be coming home from elder meetings late and exhausted and vow to get off the board but instead have to serve on a new search committee . . .

And it didn't matter, it didn't matter because Glen took his seat at the piano, and his voice wrapped Lauren in Jesus' love and lifted her and everyone else right up to the celestial gates. The band swelled in behind, and the drums and praise team kicked in. *Thank you, Lord, for*

Glen, for these people. We love you. We love you. Everyone stood up, and Lauren lost herself in the soaring praise of her favorite songs.

Except for that one chorus that didn't connect so much. Lauren focused on picking out the harmony.

"And I . . . I'm desperate for you. And I . . . I'm lost without you."

The idea of "desperation" evoked a pictorial montage of the sad life of her poor, struggling sister. So she sang the song on her behalf.

Lauren was not desperate. She was doing pretty well really. Except for Kara's room. It was good, after all these years of obedience and hard work, to be in a wide green valley of blessing.

Have you ever said that to yourself? Not the part about the room, but the part about being in a good place that is the result of all your obedience?

There is a fine line between delighting in obedience, celebrating blessing, and knowing, really knowing in the bottom of your soul that it's all sheer grace. And we often can't see it. In a season of blessing the line between thinking we deserve it just a tiny bit and reveling in 100 percent grace is just as hard to see as the pride that hides behind our desire for goodness and obedience. And yet, whether rising or hiding, our pride is perhaps the greatest blinder to seeing God. The grace we desperately need from his throne is given to the humble. "This is the one to whom I will look: he who is humble and contrite in spirit and trembles at my word" (Isa. 66:2). If we long to look on him and for him to look on us, then we have to see the pride that hides.

In 2001 we celebrated ten years of Jack's senior pastorate in a loving, committed, and creative church family in the northwest suburbs of Houston. I enjoyed the astonishing blessing of a man with a jackhammer in my living room, leading the charge to turn an anonymous gift from people in our church into a newly redecorated house, and a new knee—the blessing of a great surgeon and rehab team. Arthritis had taken out the old one, and recovery was grueling. Aside from the pain of surgery, I became very sick, and I think it took two golf foursomes of doctors to fix things.

But the greatest help, I believe, came from our elders. Over the twenty years of my illness we had twice before requested elders' prayer, but God's timing had not been ours. The men anointed my forehead and surrounded my hospital bed. It is difficult to describe the feeling of being in extreme weakness—so far down you wonder if you will ever find your way back up—and being surrounded by the strength of men who lift you up with prayers of power and faith. My misery eased enough to sleep, and the nausea faded. I would realize the full extent of God's answer in the months to come.

At summer's end I finished my second book, *Pilgrim's Progress Today*, on the deck of a tiny cabin on a glittering lake in Colorado. Zach's publisher had just released his book narrating his freshman experience in college. We celebrated together during his time off from a nearby Christian camp where he was counseling. Climbing around an old ghost town, I began to realize that my new knee was affording me more bionic mobility and relief from pain than I had enjoyed in years. It was a season of "enjoying the good life in Jerusalem," seeing God's splendor more clearly, living with creativity in the Kingdom Story—less tap-dancing, less barking for attention, less rising.

As we become sensitive to that kind of pride, we can think, *Now I get it*. And we do. We get part of it. But the pride that hides behind our desire to be good tends to be more subtle. The clues are there in our critical spirits and our worship, our self-pity and anxiety.

The previous year when my son, Zach, was a sophomore at college, we had spoken together at a mother-son retreat. My subject: The Top 10 Things I Wish I'd Known Before I Had a Son. Zach's subject: The Top Ten Things I Wish I'd Known Before I Had a Mother. Item #1 on my list: I wish I had given more encouragement and fewer "buts."

I'm a cheerleader with a "but."

I tend to cheer, "Yeah, way to go! Great job! But you could have done better if you'd just . . ." It is so hard to walk the line between holding up a vision of excellence and leveling criticism. I have so many dreams for my son and see his potential so clearly. I confessed to the moms that I'm trying to celebrate the moment more and ask if he would like suggestions later.

On his first go at a retreat talk, Zach delivered a humorous, straight-from-the-heart message telling those younger boys he wished that he had opened his life to us more and shared his thoughts, his disappointments, and dreams more. They really seemed to listen.

The next morning at breakfast with Zach, in front of God and five other people around our table, I said, "You know, Zach, you spoke so well last night. You really connected with those boys, but . . ." Zach looked at me, and everyone drew a collective breath. At which point we all burst out laughing.

Zach gave me grace. "Come on, Mom, now you've got my curiosity up."

Red-faced and apologetic, I mumbled that if any kids in the audience had ADD like he did, he could, just by virtue of standing there a few years down the road, navigating college and still breathing, cast a vision that this ADD thing could be overcome.

So well-intentioned. And such a clue to the pride that hides. *In front of all these people let me tell you that if you would just measure up to my standard for you, your performance would be so much better. Your life would be so much better.* This is just a glimpse of the pushing rather than inviting that pulses out of my pride. I have torn at the fabric of our relationship over a lost pair of pants. I can think of full-blown angry eruptions over lost projects and dirty rooms that rivaled Lauren's fury at Kara. All the heat unmitigated by the soft touch of humor.

And Zach has not been the only target in my critical crosshairs.

In his book *The Return of the Prodigal Son*, Henri Nouwen writes:

Looking deeply into myself and then around me at the lives of other people, I wonder which does more damage, lust or resentment? There is so much resentment among the "just" and the "righteous." So much judgment, condemnation and prejudice among the "saints." There is so much frozen anger among the people who are so concerned about avoiding "sin." The lostness of the resentful "saint" is so hard to reach precisely because it is so closely wedded to the desire to be good and virtuous.[40]

I think it is even worse than that. I think pride and resentment can be completely hidden by my desire to be obedient. I think that, like Lauren's running self-commentary, the leaky faucet of my heart can drip-drip criticism and contempt all day long, unless the Spirit turns it off. My strong vision of truth and the splendor of God is somehow distorted into verbal attacks upon myself and others when we don't match up to that vision.

Actually, I manage to give myself a measure of grace I don't always give others. I have not tended to think of myself as a prideful, especially a resentful person. I tend not to hold grudges. I think of myself as fairly forgiving. But the pride is there, hiding until I ask the right questions.

Am I critical? Well, hmm . . .

And here's another question: *Is my worship desperate?*

Remember Lauren thinking about her poor younger sister and how lost she was? So she sang, "I'm desperate for you" on her behalf. I've imagined that her sister worked for the IRS. She was a tax collector.

> *Two men went up into the temple to pray, one a Pharisee and the other a tax collector. The Pharisee stood up and prayed about himself: "God, I thank you that I am not like other men—robbers, evildoers, adulterers—or even like this tax collector. I fast twice a week and give a tenth of all I get." But the tax collector stood at a distance. He would not even look up to heaven, but beat his breast and said, "God, have mercy on me, a sinner!" (Luke 18:10-13 NIV)*

When I think about the Pharisees, I think, *What dirty rotten scoundrels.* But in New Testament times, the Pharisees were known for their devotion to God. Philip Yancey tells a story that highlights their commitment: When, over the Pharisees' repeated objections, Roman troops persisted in carrying standards bearing an image of the emperor as God through the streets of Jerusalem, the Pharisees fell on their faces, bared their necks, and announced they were prepared to die rather than have an idolatrous image paraded down their streets. Pilate backed down.

The Pharisees were passionately committed to the truth as they understood it. Yancey concluded that if he had lived in Jesus' time, he would have ended up a Pharisee.

Yet these were the men who leveled their constant drip-drip criticism at Jesus. "What are you doing, working on the Sabbath?" "Why are you talking to that slut?" "How come your men don't wash their hands before meals?"

"Leave them," Jesus told his disciples. "They are blind guides."

The Pharisees were so proud of their commitment to God's truth. Isn't that a good thing? The Pharisees were so legalistic—so bound up in keeping the law. Not me. I'm pretty grace-oriented.

The tax collector was desperate, and his worship was desperate. He sang, "And I'm desperate for you" from the depths of his heart. He went home justified.

How's my worship?

Is it pleasant, casual? Or is it desperate?

Am I desperate for God as a wife, a mother, a writer, a speaker?

The intensity of my need for and desire for God in worship tells me whether I am desperate for him, like the tax collector, or feeling I'm already pretty much like God, like the Pharisee.

How about my personal worship? How seriously do I take confession?

When my friend Diane taught her prayer class, she gave us a sheet entitled "Proud vs. Broken People," written by Nancy Leigh DeMoss.[41]

It is a dangerous piece of paper.

It looks simple: Two columns of contrasting characteristics, one for "Proud People," one for "Broken People." I can't say that I looked at it and thought, *Ah, that's just what I want—to be a broken person.* But as I read through the characteristics of a "broken" person, my new heart— the soft, tender heart that Jesus was rubbing with the oil of his Spirit— just wanted those things. The new heart wants what it wants, and it wants more of God.

We can't see the pride that hides any more than the nearsighted first grader on the front row can figure out what the teacher is scribbling on the chalkboard. We don't know there is any other way to see. But the prayer of confession opens the eyes of our hearts as surely as the first grader who at his first eye exam is given a pair of glasses.

The best confession is in the piercing, eye-opening moment of repentance. When my sin is hot and fresh off the fire, and God opens my eyes to see how, say, the "advice" I just offered was more of an attempt to control than love. When I turn to confession in my time alone with God, I can rarely remember my failures. In my recent memory I am a saint with a treasury of unused grace to dispense to others. This is much more a function of my poor memory than my rich character.

Praying the Psalms helps, especially David's prayers of confession. They bring me before the holy throne of grace and surface sins and attitudes I would never think to pray for. Praying through a line or two of DeMoss's list triggers specific recollections. It helps me address a calloused, insensitive spot in my new heart. Over the years I've prayed through the list many times. Made my own additions. Instead of despairing over my left-column failures, I have been invited to prayerfully imagine all that my right-column new heart can be. Here are a few items from the list:

Proud People	Broken People
Focus on the failures of others	Overwhelmed with a sense of own spiritual need
Self-righteous, critical, faultfinding spirit	Compassionate, forgiving, look for best in others
Maintain control/must be my way	Surrender control
Wounded when others are promoted and they are overlooked	Rejoice when others are lifted up
Keep people at arm's length	Risk getting close to others; loving intimately
Want to be big (my addition)	Want to be strategic for the kingdom

Again, I may be connecting unrelated dots, but what has happened in the wake of earnestly praying these requests reminds me of the story in C. S. Lewis's tales of Narnia where a selfish, prideful boy named Eustace discovers quite a pile of treasure. He leaves the company of the other children who are much too joyful and unselfish to compete with him. As he sleeps night after night atop his hoard of treasure, he becomes on the outside what his heart is on the inside: a hard, scaly, fiery-tempered dragon with a keen appetite for other dragons and humans alike.

Dragons are powerful, but they are hard to live with, and Eustace the dragon lives in his cave, growing lonelier and lonelier. He begins to see the kind of person he has become and makes the connection between being a dragon and being lonely.

Lifting his terrible dragon head, Eustace begins to weep.

Presently he sees the great lion, Aslan, who leads him to a huge well and bids him undress. Eustace scratches away at his dragon skin and manages to slither out of it. But there is always another layer of dragon skin underneath.

"You'll have to let me undress you," says the lion. Aslan's claws sink so deeply into his flesh that Eustace thinks they've gone right through his heart. The pain is breathtaking. Aslan throws him, still smarting, into the cool waters of the well. When he surfaces, he discovers that he has turned back into a real boy.

If my worship is not desperate, if I drip criticism like a leaky faucet but my prayers are serious, then Jesus will come like Aslan and, with his razor claw, rip through my proud dragon skin and release my true, naked heart.

The more his claws sink in, the more painful it is.

Many of us have felt the pain when our precious children, in whom we have invested so much of our lives, do something totally the opposite of what we've taught them. We can feel so betrayed and perhaps, at the same time, feel those claws lay open our "Oh-have-you-heard-the-latest-wonderful-thing-about-my-daughter" pride.

Many of us have worked really hard, pouring ourselves into a project that someone else comes along and slices and dices, or maybe just yawns and ignores. Part of our pain can come from those claws exposing the "aren't-you-lucky-to-have-me-on-your-team" pride that hovered just beneath the surface.

Many of us have tried to live boldly, engaging the enemy in battle, only to be laid out in a pool of our own I'm-such-a-mature-well-taught-believer-I-can-do-this blood. Realizing in our defeat that what we thought was 100 percent faith was mixed with a large dose of hey-I'm-good-enough-to-do-this self-reliance.

I left my green Colorado valley in August and descended into a year of real brokenness on each of these counts and more. I think when the towers came down on September 11, we all felt a little more vulnerable. A few weeks later our son came home from college and opened his heart to us about a personal struggle that became a family train wreck. He had been living a double life, he said, and was not the person we thought he was. He was not seeking God. He was, in fact, living what he called the "normal college lifestyle," a life very different from the one he described in his book that talked about keeping the faith in college. To me it felt like a great betrayal. Jack and I were deeply grateful for his honesty and his desire for a more authentic relationship with us, but our trust in and our dreams for our son were shattered.

In the wake of Zach's disclosures, and it truly felt like a "wake," I lost heart. I drifted around the house for weeks, like a ghost haunting the world I used to know. I grieved for my son—for all the joy and life with God he was missing and the hard road of consequences ahead. One day I'm sure Jesus will walk me through all the extra shelves in his tear cellar, and as David describes him catching our tears in his bottle, I'll see all the rows of bottles dated '01-'02 (Ps. 56:8).

Even though God had been at work in my life to deliver me from this stronghold, and I had been growing out of my Tap-Dancing Blondeness into my kingdom role as a Redemptress, our family wreck revealed so much more pride than I could ever see before. It was so unspeakably ugly that I cringed to think I was so blind to it for so long. But seeing it was also a relief, the first step toward seeking God's forgiveness and healing.

The enemy lined up an entire legion of accusers who let their fiery darts fly straight into my already wounded heart: "*You* are a pastor's wife? *You* write books on living for God and his kingdom?" I felt as if Aslan's claws ripped through my dragon skin, tore the rungs off my competitive ladder, and left me in a heap at the bottom. Videos of intense regret rolled in my head. I was flattened by guilt that made me feel like a failure as a person, a wife, a mom, a writer, a teacher. I had never felt so unworthy and overwhelmed at the things most dear to my heart.

A few weeks later an editor returned my manuscript with rewrites that no longer sounded like me and requests for extensive changes. If you've ever opened an e-mail to see someone's fat red lines through all your lovingly conceived little words, you know it can feel as if you've opened the door to the principal and the head of the PTA, and they look at you with faces furrowed with grief and tell you that some of your beautiful children are simply, well, how shall we put it . . . LOSERS, and must be dropped from their classes and sentenced to hard labor in hairnets in the cafeteria. It is Rejection with a capital R. I responded to the editor: "I feel like the tower that absorbed the impact of (Zach's confession) and still stood until yesterday. Then the cuts and rewrites of (the manuscript) collapsed just one floor of an already fragile structure, taking the whole tower down. Last night and this morning it's just rubble."

When I am wounded by rejection, and the enemy piles on his

accusations of failure, it can be a golden opportunity for God to expose the pride that hides. When God uses the hurt to reveal the true guilt of my failure, the enemy, in turn, is happy to dump truckloads of false guilt. If he can't tempt me to think, *Aren't we wonderful?* he'd just as soon take, *Aren't we horrible!* As long as my prayers are, one way or the other, all about me—my repentance, my desperate cries for help, my pleas for God to use me—it tastes just as sweet to the one who wants to devour me.

Another way to recognize the pride that hides is to ask, *Am I given to self-pity and anxiety?*

I had placed more confidence than I realized in myself and my abilities, and when I fell short, I lapsed into deep anxiety about my future. How will I be able to love well or serve with my gifts? Do I have what it takes? Will people want me? If I was so blind to my true condition, and I have failed so badly, then I have no hope that I can succeed in the future, either in relationships or ministry.

The times when we are overwhelmed with our own failure can result in a broken-hearted grief that brings us closer to God. As Chambers said, "the point of the hurt is the great point of revelation." We see the fallen depths of our own soul and our deep need for God. But when we focus on our brokenness and indulge our grief, when we want to hide because we are focused on our shame, or we fear rejection, when we cannot forgive ourselves because we have fallen so short of our longing and vision of who we want to be, we can become just as consumed with ourselves as when we are bent on rising.

In her book *How to Find Selfless Joy in a Me-First World*, professional counselor Leslie Vernick writes, "My friend Lois once told me, 'Self-love is self-love, whether it parades as pride and importance or masquerades as self-pity, worthlessness and low self-esteem. They are not opposites, but two sides of the same coin. A penny is still a penny no matter which side is up. *I* is the most important word."[42]

John Piper wrote, "Self-pity is the voice of pride in the heart of the weak . . . . The need self-pity feels does not come from a sense of unworthiness, but from a sense of unrecognized worthiness. It is the response of unapplauded pride."[43] The clues to my stronghold of pride were there in the early years of illness—feeling like I had so much to offer and yet sinking under the weight of my limitations and justifying my acceptable Christian escapes.

When I touched the true extent of my hidden pride, I found it hard to forgive myself and receive God's grace. This too can be a kind of pride that exaggerates my own misery in the face of God's power to do the very thing he came to do—release the captive Tap Dancer and bind up the broken hearts of parents. And surely a manuscript that doesn't sound like me and needs work is not the end of my dreams but rather an opportunity to grow both as a writer and a woman who embraces criticism and becomes teachable rather than bailing out or blaming others. I think my use of the word picture of the collapsing towers reflected how I was speaking from the middle of a big mess of shattered pride. I could not see the true measure of my pain in the context of the largeness of God.

John Piper reminds us, "Pride is a form of unbelief and does not like to trust in future grace. Faith admits the need for help. Pride won't. Faith banks on God to give help. Pride won't. Faith casts anxieties on God. Pride won't."[44]

The only way I have found to quiet the dark voices dumping truckloads of self-pity and sounding the alarms of anxiety is to let Christ heal the wounds of my heart, speaking the simple truths of Scripture into the depths of my soul. "He forgives your sins every one." "There is therefore now no condemnation" from God. "Why are you condemning yourself?" I imagine the battle. I see that it is the enemy who is hurling the accusations of failure and worthlessness. I turn my imagination to Christ on the cross—his passion for me, his intense desire to forgive me, and his promise never to leave or reject me. Christ on the throne—his vision for my future and his promise to share his throne with me.

Just as in the days when I had to fend off the temptation to fantasize, God's promises, sometimes spoken audibly to actually drown out the accusing voices, lifted my head and focused my vision on all that he will be and do for me in the next moment and the next and especially when I see him face to face. In my journal I wrote:

> God, you died to save me from my pride. And my screaming inadequacies. In you I realize I am sinful flesh—totally inadequate to live or love well. But I'm made in your image. I'm the object of your

wooing desire. You love me. You've redeemed me. You are the one who gave me limited abilities, my personal weaknesses, challenges within my family, thorns in my physical flesh, and all this can bring you just as much glory as I was created to give you. If you are so delighted with your own creation, then I can be too. (And P.S., you are going to look really good as you fix all this.)

As I wrote those words, I drew back in a moment of "revelation": *And isn't that the point? Isn't that what I want most with my life, for God to look good and show off his glory?*

I take him at his word, breathe deeply, and move on. I am free and clean. And I know God cherishes me, not for what I can do, but for who I *am*—his beloved. I don't want to make it look so simple. What took a few paragraphs to write took a year or more to take root at the deeper level of my exposed soul. It takes time for the truths we affirm in our heads to heal the pain of rejection and the wounded recesses of our hearts. It takes time for a celebration of grace to grow and fill all the empty places where the enemy's accusations have hollowed out our hearts, and a hidden pride had propped things up.

I'd like to dust my hands off and say, "Whew, glad that's over." But I have no illusions about discovering all the pride that hides. To C. S. Lewis's words I give a hearty amen: "From the moment a creature becomes aware of God as God and of itself as self, the terrible alternative of choosing God or self for the center is opened to it. This sin . . . is the fall in every individual life, and in each day of each individual life, the basic sin behind all particular sins: at this very moment you and I are either committing it, or about it to commit it, or repenting it."[45] I have no doubt that Aslan's claws will pierce me again, and I cringe to think that this battle with pride goes on and yet, and yet . . .

This I know: When I walked through this season of brokenness, *I could see God so much more clearly* than in my grief over the onset of rheumatoid arthritis. Twenty years ago I think my hope rested more in optimism about my circumstances than in God. *Surely medicine will help. I'll enjoy being a new mom. I'll finish my master's degree. I'll teach. Life will work.* In the more recent season I had to trust more deeply in God alone. There was no medicine for what hurt, only God.

In the first season God seemed distant. Sometimes he would reach across the blackness and give me a sweet gift of his presence, like on the plane ride home from Costa Rica. But I did not know the intimacy of his company.

In *Shattered Dreams* Larry Crabb draws a portrait of "Proud People." I found many resemblances between his picture and my younger self: "When (merely) scoldably selfish people meet a fatherly God of strict standards, their encounter with God is never intimate. It breeds . . . distance. They, too, never encounter God as their greatest pleasure."[46] The distance was there, but I couldn't see it. Being "scoldably selfish" was too much a part of me to recognize. Although I would have confessed that I loved God with all my heart, a deeply honest look at my life would have revealed that he was not my greatest pleasure.

This journey through pain has been so different. He has opened my eyes to see the depths of my need before the majesty of his throne. I've known his real presence. It doesn't mean he might not withdraw in the future to accomplish what he can only do in his absence, but what I can see of the weight and splendor of his glory is so much more Life and joy than I have known before.

Two weeks after the "rubble" e-mail I wrote my editor:

> Since September 11, the world has changed. Since [Zach's confession] my heart has changed. My pride has changed. In the mirror of my manuscript and my reaction to it, I saw that I was struggling with an unteachable spirit. I've been glorying in my own perceived strength, which was not nearly as strong as I thought.
>
> This has drawn me so much closer to the heart of Jesus Christ. I added sentences here and there that reflect that focus of deep delight and joy in him alone. They are offered with open hands.

Not only have I been able to see both God and myself more clearly, but in my journey through brokenness I received daily gifts of lavish grace and mercy. As I poured out my sorrow, he surrounded me with his wings and covered me with his feathers. I would read Scripture, and he would open my eyes and teach me at a deep heart level. He would give me glimpses into all the things besides just me that needed to be put right and how he was at work to fix them. In Larry Crabb's words I heard the voice of a gifted healer at my side as I walked through the valley. I began to catch glimpses of what my new heart was becoming in his description of "Broken People."

> But when arrogant people who know they deserve eternal misery tremble before a holy God of passionate wrath, they discover grace. They encounter the depths of God's kindness and love, a kindness and love they find nowhere else. They fall to their knees and worship Christ as their Lord and Savior and truest friend, really their only friend. They know they don't deserve a hug . . . but they get an eternal one anyway.
>
> They enter into the community of the broken, forgiven people who are hungry for all of God they can get . . . with abandon *they seek God*, alone and in the company of others.
>
> They're startled when they find their interior worlds are changing. They discover they actually want to obey God. . . . They enter their pain and discover an arrogant spirit. . . . They tremble in their unholiness before a holy God and discover how passionately they want to have a good relationship with him. Then he reveals the new way of grace. (emphasis mine)[47]

When God hurts us right out of our deceptions about ourselves, he gives us a great revelation: Godsight.

As the year progressed, I became ever more aware of another great gift God had given me: My arthritis was improving. Our elders' prayers were answered in significant measure. After going steadily downhill for over twenty years, I can hardly describe what a joy it has been to feel the vice of immobility loosen. I still deal with pain and limitation, but on a good day I can walk all the way around the block. You cannot imagine the thrill of whisking your own grocery basket down the aisle unless for years you have ridden the electric cart at a negative two miles per hour.

I am in awe of his timing. Knowing what was ahead, God began to lift a great measure of the burden of rheumatoid arthritis before Zach came home with his painful disclosures. The improvement wasn't dramatic. In fact it was so gradual I didn't fully realize what was happening. But in February I was speaking at a women's conference in Guatemala. At the end of the eleventh message in five days, I happened to glance at the empty stool I rarely had to use. I told the women, "Just look at that empty stool. A year ago I couldn't be here because of my surgery. But you prayed for me. My elders prayed for me, and here I stand." We all gave God a big cheer.

As I pray for my son, I ask God to help me not to demand seeable results. But he gives me glimpses from time to time. It is slow going, just as my own journey has been. Heart work always is. But I see Aslan stalking Zach. I see God at work showing himself, turning Zach just a bit, writing another story where he will look really good in the telling of it.

God is so much more gracious than I imagined.

In my dining room hangs my friend Lesley's shining image of the prodigal son collapsing into the embrace of his father's arms. Weary, barefoot, and half-naked, enveloped in the rich folds of his father's robe, his hands grip the father's shoulder and arm, and his head is buried in his chest. What I love is the father's face, tilted up, eyes closed, a hint of a tear slipping onto his cheek, his slight smile. I think he is saying, "Ah, my boy, my boy, my boy . . ."

Is there any more tender place to be than in the arms of a Father who loves us enough to let us live like the older brother—full of harshness, criticism, holier than thouism, unforgiveness, and jealousy? His immense sorrow over my pride and selfishness never turns to resentment. And when he exposes my heart, when I "come to my senses" like the prodigal son, he doesn't want to hear my "I'm a failure as your daughter. Maybe you could just keep me around as your screwed-up hired hand" speech. He runs to meet me and enfolds me in his embrace. He throws me a party.

Anne LaMott has said, "Grace is an acceptance of being foolish and ineffective." Larry Crabb echoes, "We are all inadequate." "We're all desperate," writes Philip Yancey, "and that is in fact the only state appropriate to a human being who wants to know God."

Pride clings to some small, unbroken fragment of obedience or talent.

Brokenness clings to the open arms of grace.

Sometimes my vision of his grace falters. A thin film of the "evil enchantment of worldliness" or the gray mist of despair will cloud my imagination. But if I lift up my eyes, I can see the City where he waits with open arms to give me the greatest grace of all . . . .

15

LIFE:
THE SEQUEL

Hope . . . is imagination put in the harness of faith.
EUGENE PETERSON

The elevator doors closed, and Tracy stepped toward the rear glass wall to take in the ascending view. Beyond the parking lots, grounds crews clipped hedges and blew off sidewalks around the medical office buildings. Farther out, the blinking lure of fast food restaurants hooked a steady flow of customers. Even from this moving height, the buckets of blossoms in front of the wholesale flower shops popped in brilliant oranges, pinks, and reds. On the ninth floor the doors opened, and Tracy turned from all the hustle and color of living to the white quiet of dying.

She knocked softly at the open door of room 906. "Jessica?"

The face slowly turned toward the door and looked at her with hooded eyes and parted lips.

"How's the pain, Jess?" Tracy touched the smooth scalp that used to be covered by the glory of Jessica's auburn mane.

"It's there, but it feels far away right now. Sometimes when the morphine can't keep up, it gets . . . close."

Tracy smiled into eyes losing the little burn of life. When Jessica had first told her, "Cancer," she had shaken her head in disbelief. "You're strong. You'll make it." The doctors had unleashed their weapons of chemical warfare, and now, six months later, it was hard to tell which had taken the greater toll, disease or poison.

Tracy wondered how anyone could think of death as just "one more turn in the circle of life." Death was an enemy. This room was a war zone where, by God's grace, all who entered had to face down the fear and love their way past it.

The two young women caught up on the few days' worth of kids and work and meds and test results since Tracy last visited. After fifteen minutes Jessica's sentences became shorter, and she asked no more questions. Tracy wondered if she should go. Jessica motioned her closer.

"I don't want you to go."

"I'm not going."

"Tracy, I want you to talk to me about heaven. And I want to lie here and listen." She surveyed the whirring, dripping machines. "I'm past the point of denial."

Tracy took Jessica's hand in hers and dropped her head. "Jess, I don't know how or where to begin. I've answered so many questions in the classes I've taught, but . . . this is so real." She paused until she could speak again. "Although so is heaven. I feel like we're standing outside the door. Inside the bridegroom is waiting, and the music has begun . . ."

"Yes, I want to imagine the wedding. Not the funeral."

Death. Our imaginations shiver at the thought. What pictures play on the screen of your imagination? Pain? Separation? The funeral?

I asked my friend Patty one day, "What do you think of when you think about death?"

She didn't hesitate. "I think about how I will look in the casket."

I looked at her. She was serious.

"Why?" she asked. "What do you think about?"

"I think about heaven." I was serious. I always think about the wedding, not the funeral.

At a relatively young age rheumatoid arthritis forced me to surrender the hope that I would find the life I long for here. With gratitude I looked back to the cross and Jesus' sacrifice. But gratitude for what God had done for me in the past did not fully engage a heart that lives in the future.

As with all of us, my capacity to imagine God and his kingdom has been greatly expanded by using my gifts in his service. As I've poured over what Scripture shows us of heaven, both for writing the last chapter of *Worldproofing* and the journey's end in Celestial City for *Pilgrim's Progress Today*, I've caught a clearer glimpse of my eternal future and all the promises I expect God to fulfill. It was like installing a Vortec V-8 engine of hope in an old, limping Volkswagen. I could gun the motor and feel the coursing energy of faith. Faith that God will give me the riches of his grace that he has promised not just in heaven, but every moment of my future that begins in the next second and stretches out to eternity.

Thornton Wilder has said, "Hope is the projection of imagination; so is despair." When rheumatoid arthritis projected the despair of so much pain and loss onto the screen of my imagination, I needed a stronger picture of hope. Hope, Eugene Peterson reminds us, "is not spinning an illusion or fantasy to protect us from our boredom or pain. It means a confident, alert expectation that God will do what he said he will do. It is imagination put in the harness of faith."[48]

Hope is imagining the holiday at the sea and letting that vision pull me through days of pain and out of the swamp of resignation and duty.

We all grieve the loss of our strength and beauty—The Way We Were when our muscles were taut and our neurons were firing. As quoted in *Time* magazine, Charles Baird, chairman of a private equity firm in Connecticut, says, "The average 75-year-old will tell you they'd give up 95% of their net worth to feel 45 again." But as I fix my eyes, deliberately turn my imagination, on Jesus and his City, I find myself not mourning getting older as much as delighting in getting closer.

I suppose I mourned getting older a long time ago. I've been on the fast track of "outwardly wasting away." Now that my friends are catching up, I watch many of them battling age with bottles and Botox. We can no longer be free to age gracefully the way our mothers did. We live in a world that worships youth and longs to fly away forever young with Peter Pan, a world where time is the enemy, stalking us like the tick-tocking crocodile. If our dreams are all on this earth, then time is a terrifying enemy, and death is the end of our dreams.

But if our dream is to know God, to see his reality in the midst of a land of fantasies and dream machines, if we dream of playing a crucial role in his kingdom, then the tick-tocking of the clock brings us closer and closer to the holiday at the sea. We can say with Paul, "For to me, to live is Christ and to die is gain. If I am to go on living in the body, this will mean fruitful labor for me. Yet what shall I choose? I do not know! I am torn between the two: I desire to depart and be with Christ, which is better by far; but it is more necessary for you that I remain in the body" (Phil. 1:21-24 NIV). If we really see the wonder of Christ and his kingdom, we will feel torn. If we don't, we can't even imagine what Paul has seen.

But we are invited to imagine it.

I wonder if we're in for much of a trip down the aisle. The kingdom of the heavens is in the air all around us. In the same way we read, "Suddenly an angel was standing there," so many times in Scripture, I think we will step through the "dark glass" and be right there. "Absent from the body, present with the Lord."

At the conclusion of *The Return of the King* Frodo says good-bye to his friends. He hugs each in turn, lastly Samwise. They have finished their quest, saved the Shire. The sweet taste of victory has been seasoned with the bitterness of foolish decisions and even betrayal. Their tears flow from the deep places in their souls where they have learned to forgive much and love much. Frodo boards the ship headed for the light of the distant shore, and as he looks back upon his friends, he can't help it. The pain in his eyes turns to joy. He tilts his head just a bit as if to say, *I'm off now on my adventure*. The ship sails out of the harbor and is engulfed in the brilliant light. It is the movie clip I want played at my funeral.

Don't cry, my friends. You taste my departure more than I do. You watch me leave. I see the City of light coming closer and closer, the new Jerusalem Jesus promised us, "which is coming down out of heaven from my God" (Rev. 3:12 NIV).

At the end of our Story (Rev. 21), God invites us to imagine that stunning event. An angel shows John the heavenly city "coming down out of heaven from God, having the glory of God, its radiance like a most rare jewel, like a jasper, clear as crystal" (v. 11). The city will come down out of heaven, shining like diamonds, bathed in the Shekinah glory of God. I wonder if it will come all the way down to earth, or if, as some scholars suggest, it might hang suspended over the earth, perhaps over Israel. Imagine our newly recreated earth rotating underneath it.

"And the one who spoke with me had a measuring rod of gold to measure the city and its gates and walls. The city lies foursquare; its length the same as its width. And he measured the city with his rod, [1,500 miles]. Its length and width and height are equal" (vv. 15-16). Imagine our heavenly hometown laid out in 3-D with layers of streets and dwellings prepared especially for us stretching as far as from Maine to Florida and the Atlantic to Colorado and then that high again.

I like the detail of the angel's measuring rod. So many people today believe that only what we can see, hear, touch, smell, and taste is really "real." Scientists especially like to make the point that if something can't be measured, it isn't real. I think God wanted to make the point: This city is as real as it gets.

Imagine all the people on a newly recreated earth looking up and seeing the rainbow-foundationed city glowing in the sky, something like the view from the street or the back porch described in chapter 1.

"The wall was built of jasper, while the city was pure gold, clear as glass" (v. 18). "And the street of the city was pure gold, transparent as glass" (v. 21). Can you imagine translucent gold? The atomic composition of things will be so "other." Light suffuses everything. I suppose it shouldn't surprise us. A city that is home to the "Father of heavenly lights" will dazzle us with fiery stones—a color and brightness we'll be strong enough to see.

"The foundations of the wall of the city were adorned with every kind of jewel" (v. 19)—sapphire blue, emerald green, golden topaz, carnelian red, amethyst purple, and more—all the colors of the rainbow. Imagine, suspended in the air, how that might look. A city as an everlasting rainbow—living proof of the God who keeps his promises, like the reminder of God's other promise long ago.

"And I saw no temple in the city, for its temple is the Lord God the Almighty and the Lamb" (v. 22). Can you imagine a city with no churches? No temple? No more sacred building over here, secular establishments over there. All of life is sacred. Everything is worship—business, schools, recreation, government—whatever goes on there, all the walls and separation will be done with. Imagine a community and a life with that wholeness and integrity we so *long* for.

We see God's stunning majesty reflected in the mountains and rivers made by his hand. But all our cities are man-made. We have caught glimpses of the beauty of buildings designed by God (the tabernacle, the temple he showed to Ezekiel), and we have seen beautiful cities laid out by men such as Napoleon (Paris) and Pierre Charles L'Enfant (hired by George Washington to create the master plan for Washington, D.C.). Imagine a planned community that will dazzle with the beauty of the designing mind of God and shimmer with his visible radiance.

"The glory of God gives it light, and its lamp is the Lamb. By its light will the nations walk, and the kings of the earth will bring their glory into it" (vv. 23-24). "Nations will walk," "kings will bring"—perhaps, as some scholars think, the New Jerusalem will be on the earth, and we will be the "nations"; or perhaps we're being given a glimpse of a world to come with more nations and kings on the earth below while we enjoy our dwelling places in the city in the sky.

John tries to wrap words around a fantastic new setting for the sequel to the Story of Life. But, as with our part of the Story, the setting is never the main thing. For the longest time I've made that mistake about heaven. I always thought primarily of heaven as a setting—a place far better than "the other place," or this place. I concentrated on what it *looks* like—the breathtaking beauty. And it will be that. But more than that, I've discovered that the setting is the backdrop for relationships and action.

What can we discover about the characters and the plot in this sequel to Life—The Story?

"The throne of God and of the Lamb will be in it, and his servants will worship him" (Rev. 22:3). "And they will reign forever and ever" (v. 5). At the beginning of Revelation, a promise is given to those who overcome. "The one who conquers and who keeps my works until the end, to him I will give authority over the nations" (Rev. 2:26). We are back before the throne of our radiant lover and King who invites us to sit with him there.

"Authority," "reign," influence over nations. God dreams a large role for us in the sequel to the Story. Twice in Revelation the Lamb is praised, "for you were slain, and by your blood you ransomed people for God from every tribe and language and people and nation, and you have made them a kingdom and *priests to our God, and they shall reign on the earth*" (Rev. 5:9, 12). We will be priests and co-regents over people who need shepherding, who need our influence and leadership.

How do you respond to the prospect of that measure of leadership and responsibility? Do you feel ready to reign?

My imagination for heaven used to be a vague picture of singing and worshiping and resting. What about yours? Did you think it would be eating? Strolling around with plenty of time to do whatever we want, like a permanent vacation? Like retirement without the golf? Maybe *with* the golf?

"Heaven as reigning?" my friend Roberta mused. She sighed. Roberta spends well over forty hours a week scaling a Sisyphusian mountain of paperwork—new stacks always arriving before the old ones are ready to depart. "To me heaven will be like standing at the top of a slope, the sun sparkling off the fresh powder just waiting to be skied." Not that heaven is Snowmass, but rest and recreational joy beyond imagining.

And I believe she is right. God has given to those who believe in his Son a promise of entering his rest (Heb. 4:1). What refreshes your heart? Skiing, white-water rafting? Watching *Braveheart* movies that blaze with God's redemptive theme, or pelicans dive-bombing for their dinner? The R&R of heaven will be unimaginably more restful. The Good Shepherd will lead you to a place that thoroughly restores your soul. But, as in this part of the Story, I believe the rest restores us for the challenge that awaits—the reigning that, with worship, seems to be the registered occupation of everyone in Revelation 21.

What does it mean "to reign"?

Isn't the basic idea to be a person of influence? To be in relationship with others who follow your influence and example? Isn't it clear that being a person of influence is not God's far distant dream for us but his earnest desire right now?

You are a "light," "a city set on a hill," that can't be hidden, Jesus said.

Jesus and Paul invited every believer to follow their examples, which meant to live in such a way as to set an example.

Paul exhorted Titus to set an example for the younger men and encouraged Timothy himself, the younger man, to set an example.

We hear the basketball star who protests, "I don't want to be anybody's example." And before we wag our heads, we ask ourselves, "Do we want to live as persons of influence?"

If people are watching us and following us, like the basketball star, we are examples. Every dad is an example. Every mom is a woman of influence. Every person who shares an opinion or casts a vision of possibilities with the hopes of influencing the ideas and actions of others (and who doesn't?) is recruiting followers.

Every person ransomed by the blood of Jesus Christ shares a royal destiny. We "will reign upon the earth."

We can ignore or even shrink back from this destiny. We can indulge our Cosmic Blondeness and "just want to get a good time out of my life." Just go to work, go to church, and watch TV. But reigning is the future. If we are Christ's people, he wants us to reign. So how do we imagine that future and think backwards to the present? What does this mean for me today?

I think it means, "Be a man . . . be a woman whose daily decisions are shaped by a vision and a passion for living and reigning in God's kingdom now." And in the same breath I have to ask, how often does my vision of becoming a woman of kingdom influence motivate my daily choices? Paul admonished the Corinthians to let the saints (not necessarily the elders, just the rank and file *saints*) judge over disagreements among believers in the church. And he appeals to this very motive: Don't you know you're going to judge the world and even angels? "If you are to judge the world, are you not competent to judge trivial cases?" (1 Cor. 6:2 NIV). No commentator I've read seems to have this verse completely figured out, but if you've served in churches, you can empathize with Paul's frustration.

Have you ever been involved in a dispute among believers? The color of the new church carpet is a hill to die on. The choice of curriculum for the Women Who Exegete in Greek and Hebrew study group creates a smoldering grudge between the Montagues and the Capulets. What we think is all about ministry is far too much about validation. "For crying out loud," Paul is saying, "you are validated! You are chosen! You will rule over the world! In light of that vision, this stuff is so trivial!" We need the reigning perspective.

Embracing our roles as Kingdom Redemptors and Redemptresses wears Jack and me out. Sometimes he smiles at me and says, "I think I'll quit and go sell shoes." And I say, "Yeah, let's just go blend in among the masses at the mega-church." Which is no commentary on either selling shoes or going to Seventeenth Baptist Church, but just our wishful vision of a comfortable Christian retreat from the slings and arrows of life on the frontlines where we aspire to be people of influence. When we recover our perspective, we are reminded: These are all twists and turns in the plot of the Story where the real point is seeking and finding a God who wants to make us like Jesus—in other words, the kind of people he can set free to reign in his universe.

Some people respond to the vision of reigning not with angst or indifference, but with a few too many stars in their eyes. Their religions lay out a detailed prescription for reigning. If you make a missionary commitment and raise your children a certain way, you will attain this level on the org chart of ruling the universe. And it motivates people.

I'm glad the Bible doesn't lay it out like that. Because all the other Tap Dancers and I would be scrambling, just like James and John, to see who gets the throne next to Jesus.

We will reign. We will share God's throne.

The plot should matter. The expectation of reigning ought to motivate us to move in that direction now. All our daily kingdom choices go with us. When we join that joyful assembly, we'll wish we had gone all out. The colicky babies and domineering bosses, the offenses we couldn't forgive and the dreams that shattered—we will wonder that

we let any of it distract our imagination from Godsight. We will immediately see reality so clearly. We will wish we had another opportunity
to get it right. And we will have Life: The Sequel.

But it won't be the same. It will be with eyes wide open. Sight, not
faith. Now is the only time to take the risk.

Not only will we take our gifts and our growth with us, but even
our suffering goes with us, preparing us to reign. In 2 Corinthians Paul
said, "For our light and momentary troubles are achieving for us an
eternal glory that far outweighs them all" (4:17 NIV). In years past I read
this verse and thought, *Light and momentary troubles!* *"God, are you
taking me seriously?"*

In the kingdom all my suffering with rheumatoid arthritis—the
agony, the surgeries, the energy drain, the pocketbook drain, even the
pangs of never being able to wear cute, strappy little sandals—all that
and a broken family will seem like light and momentary troubles. I told
my friend Carol, "One day, 300 years into the kingdom, we will have
tea beside the River of Life, and my sorrows and your grief over JP's
guilt and imprisonment will truly seem light and momentary." Or
maybe it won't be 300 years. Maybe it will be just three days.

Think of your greatest grief. One hundred years from now it will
seem light and momentary. Not because your suffering is a small thing
to God, and not just because whatever we endure here for seventy or
eighty years here can't compare with what we will enjoy for millions of
years there, but also because you will live day by day with the glory
achieved by that suffering—the weight of moral authority, the ability
to influence with a depth of understanding, and so much more.

A story told about Emperor Constantine paints a poignant picture
of what is meant by "a weight of glory" that far exceeds our momentary troubles. When Constantine declared Christianity the official reli-
gion of the Roman Empire, he ordered the Christians who were
imprisoned for their faith released and their chains to be weighed.
Then they were given an amount of gold equal to the weight of their
chains.

Somehow God converts all our suffering into something worth living for. Ashes into a crown of beauty, mourning into the oil of gladness,

and a spirit of despair into a garment of praise (Isa. 61:3). We'll enjoy the person we've become for eternity, and so will Jesus.

<hr />

We can perhaps imagine a "city" and "reigning." But the best part of heaven is the great intangible: the knowing.

Think of the time you've been in the most beautiful, exotic setting or immersed in important work or thrilling adventures. Our heart's greatest desire is to enjoy it with people. But not just any people, people whom we know and who mean a great deal to us, kindred spirits who truly understand us. Part of the joy of visiting the British Museum was walking with Zach among the colossal Egyptian statues hewn out of the rock and hauled home to England and joking that we could hear the British archeologists stumbling upon these treasures and wanting to share *their* adventures: "Great Scot! Margaret has just got to see this." "Oh, the queen, her majesty will love this." Out came the giant hacksaws.

What of all these longings we have to be known—to be noticed and chosen and cherished forever? In heaven we will be. Can you imagine the needle on your tank resting on "full"? Every day. Life with no ache? Can you imagine Jesus himself erasing all the yearnings? The main thing, the best thing about heaven is that "the throne of God and of the Lamb" will be there. We will be where Jesus is. I try to imagine that unity—what a new order of things without a moment's rejection will be like. It's a challenge. The unlimited affirmation, the eternal YES of a God who will forever affirm and enjoy me makes me laugh in anticipation.

All our seeking will be face to face. "And this is eternal life, that they know you the only true God, and Jesus Christ, whom you have sent" (John 17:3).

How can we delight in the prospect of a future in heaven, but not in spending time with Jesus now?

Eternal life is not mainly about dying and going to a "place" called heaven. It's not a celestial extension of our all-about-me culture where the five people you meet in heaven unfold to you the meaning of your life while God (he's around here somewhere) is busy running the universe. It's about living now and always close to Jesus, drinking in his love and beauty. It's sharing our moments with him—celebrating with him, living from the heart with him. I've discovered that Revelation talks about this kind of intimacy in the language of names and naming.

"The one who conquers . . . I will write on him the name of my God . . . and my own new name." I've wondered, what does it mean to give someone a name? It means you know her, and you give her an identity.

When we were deciding what to name our son, we chose Zachary in large part because I was so sick, and my pregnancy was so risky, and we wanted our baby to be "remembered by the Lord," the Hebrew meaning of Zechariah. We wanted him to grow up knowing that even before he was born, he was given the identity of one whom God thought about and protected. I wanted to give that legacy to my son because I have taken strength and identity from my name, Lael, Hebrew for "belonging to God." And that is my prayer for him still: "God, please remember my boy."

In Revelation 22:4 (NIV) John writes, "They will see his face, and his name will be on their foreheads." I've wondered, what does it mean to wear someone's name?

Here in Texas we have a high school tradition where a guy gives his date a mum corsage for the homecoming football game. Back when I was in school, your basic mum was a single flower with a few ribbon streamers in your school colors. But nowadays that look is so '60s. Today's mum is at least a double fresh flower or about five or six silks, so loaded with ribbons and footballs and teddy bears and bells and whistles and blinking neon lights that the girls have to fasten them with duct tape to their shoulders and hand-carry the twenty streamers and footballs and cowbells.

At the game I watch them heaving their load up and down the bleachers, like Marley's ghost dragging his chains into Scrooge's bedroom. But, unlike Marley's ghost, the girls are all smiles because one feature of mums past and present remains the same: The *name* of their date or the number of their football-playing boyfriend is plastered in big glittering letters on the streamers. So that all the world knows: *I've got this man. Or I've got this woman.* It identifies the girl with the guy, gives that idea of belonging, just like a bride takes the name of her husband. *I belong to you. You belong to me.* Only the mums say it with less subtlety.

People wear names all the time, wanting to share in the identity of those names, hoping that something about the good names will rub off on them. People love to wear T-shirts emblazoned with sports teams, rock groups, movies, Disneyland. When we wear them, what are we saying? *I'm hot like these guys.*

In some symbolic or real sense, we conquerors will wear the name of Jesus on our foreheads. Somehow people will see his name when they look at our faces. My radical friend Charlene says, "See, we'll all have tattoos!"

The remarkable thing is, Jesus wears our name—engraved on the palms of his hands. Through Isaiah God says, "See, I have engraved you on the palms of my hands" (49:16 NIV). He remembers us. He identifies with us. Our names are engraved right next to the nail print. We belong to him. He belongs to us. Heaven will be the fullness of that intimacy.

The same message is spoken in Revelation 2:17 (NIV): "To him who overcomes . . . I will also give him a white stone with a new name written on it, known only to him who receives it."

Jesus knows our names. He thinks of us by name. Prays for us by name. In heaven he will give each of us a new name that reflects our unique identity. He honors and celebrates our uniqueness. In heaven we will never feel like the odd one out or the misfit. Never again will we be left standing outside the sacred circle, longing to get in.

What does it mean for someone to give you a name that only the two of you know? Intimacy. The names are a sign of secret affection. Secret names have a meaning uniquely special to the lovers who share them. Jack and I have secret names for one another. To two people deeply delighted with the intimacy of their relationship, secret names are a precious symbol of unity, a joyful *knowing*.

In Revelation 3:5 (NIV) I discovered my favorite picture of the intimacy we will enjoy in heaven: "He who overcomes will, like them, be dressed in white. I will never blot out his name from the book of life, but will acknowledge his name before my Father and his angels." This "acknowledging" sounds like Ephesians 5: "Christ loved the church and gave himself up for her to make her holy . . . and to *present* her to himself as a radiant church, without stain or wrinkle or any other blemish" (v. 27 NIV, emphasis mine). It sounds like a wedding.

To present is to stand alongside. Perhaps Christ will stand beside us and present us, acknowledge our names, to his Father and his angels. That's always the high point of a wedding, isn't it? Now I present to you Mr. and Mrs. Jack Arrington. Do you remember the thrill?

I can imagine Jesus standing beside us, radiant, clothed in spotless white, and presenting us by name to the Father and all the heavenly hosts. Delighting in our beauty. Bursting with pride over the persons we've become. Our feelings for each other will soar beyond words to express.

Let's not lose sight of our identity on this side of that moment. I am not a teacher or a "rheumatoid arthritis patient." I am not even at the core of my soul a mother or a wife as much as I am part of the Princess Bride, betrothed to my King, awaiting the wedding. I am the Redemptress Bride, a woman forgiven much who has much to offer others in Jesus' name. And you are too. Jesus will present you to the Father and all the angels by a name that expresses all that you are and acknowledges the beauty and person of glory you are becoming.

The knowing will be like a wedding. After the presentation, our lives together really begin. The intimacy of heaven will be greater than the best sex.

Okay, this is where we need all the imagination we can muster. Jesus tells us that we won't be married or given in marriage. Not because God wants to limit us or take something precious away. On the other hand, some scholars believe that heaven will be like mass marriage. The same delight and transparency that we enjoy in marriage we will share with everyone. Especially Jesus. Our capacity for the joy of intimacy won't be diminished but expanded. We shall "know fully, even as [we are] fully known."

We'll finally understand how to truly experience and cherish and celebrate each other, as well as God. I'll think of all those things to say and do for others that now either don't occur to me until too late or not at all. We won't struggle to yield the right to be right, or give others the credit, or serve their needs over our own. The strongholds of